MOM, INC.

MOM, INC.

Parenting as if You Mean Business

CYNTHIA MACGREGOR

TAYLOR TRADE PUBLISHING
Dallas • Lanham • Boulder • New York • Toronto • Oxford

First Taylor Trade Publishing edition 2005

This Taylor Trade Publishing paperback edition of *Mom, Inc.* is an original publication. It is published by arrangement with the author.

Published by Taylor Trade Publishing
An imprint of The Rowman & Littlefield Publishing Group, Inc.
4501 Forbes Boulevard, Suite 200
Lanham, MD 20706

Distributed by NATIONAL BOOK NETWORK

Library of Congress Cataloging-in-Publication Data

MacGregor, Cynthia.
    Mom, Inc. : parenting as if you mean business / Cynthia MacGregor.—
1st Taylor Trade Pub. ed.
        p. cm.
    Includes index.
    ISBN 1-58979-177-0 (pbk. : alk. paper)
    1. Mothers—Psychology. 2. Mothers—Attitudes. 3. Mother and child.
    4. Parenting. I. Title. HQ759.M2983 2005
        306.874'3—dc22   2004019692

∞™ The paper used in this publication meets the minimum requirements of American National Standard for Information Sciences—Permanence of Paper for Printed Library Materials, ANSI/NISO Z39.48-1992.

Manufactured in the United States of America.

For Laurel . . . of course!
Though she's doing a fine job already,
even without the help of a book.

And also dedicated to the memory of Yvonne.

CONTENTS

INTRODUCTION

It's 3:00 p.m. in your office. You've called a departmental meeting. You go through the usual formalities, hear from the usual complainers (and deal with them in true corporate fashion), assign some tasks and some other projects, listen to reports, deal with requests and questions, ask a few questions of your own, and call the meeting to an end in plenty of time for those who have to catch the 5:28 commuter train to be on board as usual.

It was a tiring meeting, a challenging meeting—though isn't that par for the course? But you know you've accomplished something; you know the various projects you're shepherding are going along as they should be. Your work in the office is challenging but rewarding. Your professional life is tiring—sometimes exhausting—but yet it's fulfilling.

But . . . tiring? Did I mention tiring? Yes, I did. Right now, as you slip your two-inch pump off your corporately tired foot, you stretch, yawn, and look forward to the end of the day, when—in only a few minutes now—you can leave the office and the stress of work and go home to . . .

To what? To more stress? To the hassles of sibling rivalry, worse than the infighting of rival managers vying to be recognized as deserving of the next promotion? To the stress of mediating family hassles, more taxing on your nerves than any labor dispute? To "It's not my turn to do the dishes" or "It's his turn to take out the garbage," more contentious than any task-related job quarrels?

Do you really want to go home? As tiring as the office is, at least it's well run. Yes, there are situations that have to be dealt with, personality conflicts that need to be worked out, workers who need to be coaxed or cajoled or sometimes even threatened into doing their best, and deadline pressures when a last-minute project runs late. Yes, it's an awful minefield. But still, it's far more peaceful—and manageable—than what you face when you get home.

Your older son doesn't want to clean his room. Your daughter blasts her music at top volume. She seems determined to destroy your eardrums all on her own and make enemies of your neighbors at the same time. Your younger son finds every excuse in the world to avoid the few chores you think are perfectly reasonable for a boy of six. (Naturally, he doesn't agree and accuses you of being involved in the slave labor trade.)

And your husband isn't the help you know he should be.

If only your home life were as easy to organize as your work life is.

But it can be. Have you ever tried running your home life like a business? Have you ever tried parenting CEO-style?

No, it's not the perfect panacea. You'll always have malcontents, dissenters, disturbers, and other disharmonious types. There's no book—including this one—that can promise you instant happiness and perfect bliss.

If you find one, you'll know they're lying.

I'm not lying. And I'm not promising you total freedom from the hassles and unpleasantness of parenting.

But this book *can* make parenting a whole lot easier. Just follow the corporate model. And turn the organization and management of your home into a corporately structured entity.

You'll be surprised at the results.

Right now, it's nearly 5:00. You're stretching your toes for the last time before cramming them back into your tight and uncomfortable shoes. Your life as a mother is often as tight and uncomfortable as those shoes are. You like being a mother. You love your kids. But you sure wish things were . . . different.

Resolve—right now, before you catch that 5:28 train to the suburbs or get in your car for the drive to your cul-de-sac or catch the subway uptown to your apartment on the Upper West Side—to start running your household, your home, like a business. When you tell your kids, "Clean your rooms now. I mean business!" do you literally mean it? You should! You mean business in a very literal sense.

Starting today, you mean to run your home very much like a business. You mean to rule your household as if you were its chief executive officer. (Well, aren't you? You may have a co-CEO, but that doesn't diminish *your* power!) Starting today, you're going to treat your kids as if they are underlings in the power hierarchy (well, aren't they?) and as if they have to answer to you (well, don't they?!) and as if you wield the reins in this corporate structure. And they are going to fall in line and behave in the corporate model.

Well, not totally. Kids will be kids, after all. And, let's face it, the corporate model includes malcontents, snitches, slackers, and others who have to be dealt with.

Nobody ever said that running a corporation is easy.

And nobody ever said that running a family on the corporate model would be easy either.

But I bet it's a whole lot easier than what you're trying now.

Do you doubt me?

I don't blame you.

But try it my way. Or at least, read the rest of this book. And then tell me if you don't believe that running a family on the corporate model will be a hell of a lot easier than whatever plan you're currently using—if you have a plan at all.

Be the CEO of your family. It's a business. And you're the head of it. You're the CEO of Mom, Inc. You deserve respect for your talents, your knowledge, your brainpower, your handling of personal crises. (Hell, doesn't it sound like another day at the office?) And you *have* those talents, those skills, that brainpower. You've got a plethora of corporate abilities and knowledge already on tap. Why not put it all to use in your most challenging job of all: parenting.

There's a family waiting for you to take the corporate reins and be its CEO. Go to it!

1

THE MOST IMPORTANT
JOB YOU'LL EVER HAVE

When you're seeking a new position in your career, you first prepare a resume to present to whoever's doing the hiring. That may be someone in human resources in a large firm, the office manager of a smaller concern, or your best friend's Uncle Kenny's neighbor, who's looking for a new sales manager. It may even be a blind box ad or fax number—a faceless, nameless entity who'll know all about you while you don't even know the name of, or any other info about, the company you're applying to.

There's a funny thing about resumes. Though creating them is an endeavor that buffaloes many an otherwise competent individual, they serve a very real purpose *for the job applicant,* not just for the employer: they help you remember all the things you've done, education you've acquired, and other relevant experiences you've had that make you well suited for the job.

If you're like most people, you probably don't have one standard resume that you give or send to all prospective employers. You probably re-create your resume from one job application to the next, subtly reshaping the information you offer, slanting it to put forward what you suspect will be your best foot for this particular job, this particular company.

As you go through this process, you mentally scratch your head, trying to think of the different things you've done, perhaps even the different courses you've taken, that would best reflect your competency for the particular position you're applying for. If the job requires that you do a certain amount of public speaking, and you've addressed groups on the subject of birdwatching in conjunction with your hobby, you may even find that your hobby helps qualify you for the job.

Often, by the time you've finished crafting your resume, you have much more confidence in your ability to do the job, should you get it, than you had initially. Isn't it wonderful what a resume can do? It not only can persuade a prospective employer of your suitability—it can convince *you* too!

As you mentally press the rewind button on your life and go back through your various experiences, trying to think of what you've done, what you've learned, what you've experienced that make you suitable for the task at hand, you realize just how much there is to your credit.

Too bad that undertaking motherhood doesn't require your first submitting a resume! As you listed everything you ever did that helped make you ready for what is arguably the most important job of your life, you'd start with all the times you "minded" your younger siblings, and you'd add in all your babysitting experience . . . but why stop there?

Your business life qualifies you too!

Your business life? Yes!

Hasn't your career taught you such skills as delegating responsibility, being a good supervisor, encouraging others to do their best, learning when to trust and when to be suspicious, and myriad others that we'll get into later in this book?

These are all skills you'll need, and use, in parenting.

This most important job is one that doesn't require you first submit an application, prepare a resume, take a test to qualify, or get a license. Yet in spite of that, many of the business skills you've acquired in the course of your career thus far are going to come in very handy. Handier than you now realize.

What *has* your career experience been? There are damn few women anymore who go right from school into marriage and become stay-at-home wives and then mothers without working. Whether you worked up till the middle of your pregnancy or right through it, and whether you now work full-time, part-time, or not at all, you almost certainly have had some experience in the workforce.

And whether you were an upper-level executive, middle management, or a secretary or sales rep, you have some idea of the workings of the corporate culture and the skills needed to survive in it. Even if your career has been elsewhere than in the standard business world, you probably have a pretty good idea of how a business is run and have acquired many of the needed skills.

They'll look fine on your "resume" for parenting.

Take those skills you learned as the Big Boss, or a department head, or a small cog in the machinery of industry, whether you worked in the corporate culture or for a non-profit or behind the counter at a local store, and *run your family like a business.*

Even if you married right out of school and "retired" before ever becoming a nine-to-fiver, or worked on a one-woman farm and totally escaped the corporate culture and the experience of either having a boss or being a boss, you surely have some knowledge of the business world, either vicariously through your husband's, parents', or friends' experiences, or as a result of part-time jobs or summer jobs you yourself held while in school.

Besides which, you've been exposed through newspapers, magazines, and TV to the concepts of corporate leadership. Corporate leadership is a wonderful model for parenting.

Though there are lessons to be learned both from the heads of Fortune 500 companies and from the owners of startup or very small companies, the best model is the head of a small-to-medium company, one who "wears many hats" in the course of the work week and is particularly involved in the day-to-day activities of her company. But above all, a good corporate leader—no matter the size of the enterprise—knows how to keep a firm hand on the helm, motivate the people below her, empower them while remaining empowered herself, and keep control of the company and the people who work there.

Isn't that a good description of a successful mother?

How many times have you seen a child run roughshod over his mom? Just to take one of the most common examples, a mother goes into a store with her small child, who sees a toy, a comic book, or a box of cookies that he wants. He asks for it. She says no. He asks more loudly. She says no more loudly. He gets belligerent. She threatens him with a time-out if he doesn't stop it. He starts to scream.

And she gives in, rather than let him make a scene and embarrass her in public.

Who's the boss in that family?

Not the mom. She's not keeping a firm hand on the helm.

Take one more example. This time the child is an eleven-year-old. The mother is trying to get dinner ready, plan her menus for next week, and make notes toward a speech that she needs to deliver at the PTA meeting. The eleven-year-old is supposed to be doing her homework and setting the table. Instead she's playing a video game. Mom tells the child to stop playing and take care of her homework and chores. The child says she'll be done with the game in a minute. But ten minutes later, she's still playing, her homework isn't getting done, and the table hasn't been set yet. Mom reminds Daughter, sounding a trifle annoyed. Daughter sounds more than a trifle annoyed in her response: "Give me a minute!" She makes it seem *Mom* is being unreasonable. Ten minutes later, when Mom again calls out to Daughter in the living room, the child says, "I don't have that much homework anyhow."

Does Mom say, "Well, pause the game, set the table, and start your homework, please. If there's that little to do, you'll be able to get back to your game quickly"? No. Rather than get involved in another hassle with Daughter, she lets her be, resolving to get on her about her homework right after dinner. And Mom sets the table herself. (It's too bad the chops got overcooked while she was laying out napkins, plates, and utensils.)

Who's running *that* family?

Not the mom!

What would a good corporate manager do?

Well, first of all, she'd know what everyone under her is supposed to be doing. Second, she'd make sure *they* know what they're supposed to be doing. And third, she'd make sure they did it.

To begin with, she'd try to lead them into *wanting* to accomplish their tasks on time. You may object that few people enjoy working. I say that's not so. Many people do enjoy working. But even those who don't—or those who do but are faced with an unpleasant task—enjoy having the task behind them. If you *know* you have to do something—whether it's writing a dull and boring report at work or firing someone who hasn't been performing well, or whether it's homework or setting the table—facing the knowledge that you have to do it is like carrying a twenty-pound stone on your back. And having it done and behind you and over with is like no longer having to carry that weight.

Just as good employees can be shown that it's best to do unpleasant or boring tasks and get them out of the way, kids can learn the same lesson.

But sometimes that isn't enough to motivate them. In that case, there are other ways. For a particularly odious task, there's always the possibility of promising a reward at the task's completion. Some may call that bribery, but it's really a workable rewards system. After all, isn't that what corporate bonuses, Employee of the Month plaques, parking places of honor (nearest the entrance in a large parking lot), and other incentives are about?

There's a difference between promising a reward for completing a particularly difficult or disagreeable task and bribing a child with sweets for simply making his bed every morning.

What *doesn't* a good corporate manager do?

Let her employees take charge of the company.

We were talking about keeping your hand on the helm. A very large part of that is letting the child know that you're the boss. When you give that four-year-old who's acting bratty a comic book or box of cookies just to keep him from making a scene in the store, you're letting him know *he's* the boss. When you let your eleven-year-old get away with playing her video game instead of doing her homework or setting the table, you're ceding leadership to her, too.

Being a boss isn't always a fun job. Neither is being a mom. But if you *tell* the kids you're the boss, *act like* you're the boss, and *follow through* like you're the boss, your kids will believe it. The four-year-old who screams to get cookies will grow into a six-year-old who screams or throws things or acts out in other unpleasant ways to get what he wants.

And God help you when that child becomes a teenager.

He sets a bad example for the rest of the kids too.

It's true that sometimes you have to let your child make a bad decision and see what the result of his course of action is. But there are also times when that isn't practical. The child who is allowed to goof off instead of studying and, as a result, earns an F on her spelling test the next day may learn a lesson, or she may not care that she failed the test, not even after what you say when shown the graded test. And the child who is acting out in the antiques store and in danger of knocking some expensive china figurines to the floor is not the one who will suffer most directly as a consequence of his action. Your wallet will bear the brunt of that unfortunate tantrum, even if the child faces disciplinary consequences too.

Similarly you might let a child eat his fill of Halloween candy after a cautionary talk on the possible consequences, hoping that if he gets a tummyache he'll learn a lesson. But if he habitually eats poorly—too many sweets, no veggies, too many fried foods, and poor-choice snack foods—and suffers no noticeable ill effects, he'll be doing his health no favor, yet he's not learning a lesson. This child needs guidance.

A good corporate-style mother knows when to let her children make poor choices and learn from the consequences, and when it's appropriate to step in and intervene.

A good corporate manager knows that one bad apple is a bad influence on the rest of the organization. If one salesperson can get away with playing computer solitaire instead of calling prospects, the others will want to try it, or will simply resent the fact that they have to work while he goofs off. Soon you have an unproductive department.

And if one child can get away with not setting the table, soon her brother won't want to take out the garbage and her other brother will refuse to do the dishes.

A good corporate manager tries to lead her employees into being willing to do their work. If they're not actually eager to accomplish their tasks, they'll be eager to get them done and over with. At very least, they'll accept the fact that the tasks have to be done—if for no better reason than because the boss says so.

Of course, a corporate manager has the luxury of, in an extreme, being able to fire an uncooperative, unproductive employee. That's an option you don't have. You can't trade in a sullen fourteen-year-old for a cheerful teen or fire a family member who's lazy and replace her with one who'll do all her chores willingly.

Fortunately, there are ways to elicit cooperation from kids. This book will discuss them. But the most important thing of all is to make sure they know that *you're the boss*. If they don't believe that, nothing else is going to work. And to get them to believe it, you have to act the part. You have to really take charge. Not by micro-managing, and not by standing over each child while he does everything he's supposed to.

That's not the way to get them to complete tasks on their own. And besides, you'll never get your own work done that way. But you do need to ensure that the kids understand who's in charge. That when you say, "No cookies today," you mean it. And when you say, "Set the table and start your homework," you mean that too.

Because you're the boss.

There are various ways of motivating employees and kids alike. We've already discussed that briefly, including showing them how good it feels to get that twenty-pound stone off their backs. We've also touched on the rewards system employed in the corporate culture, where plaques and privileges, medals, and other honors await the employee who is most productive, most inventive, most courteous, most loyal, or simply best all-around.

The sales charts and similar graphs an office employs have their counterparts in a home environment as well. In an office, these charts may show how each salesperson is doing compared with the others, or how a department's output compares this month with last, or who is deserving of special commendation.

In your home, too, displaying a record of accomplishments for the kids to be proud of is one means of motivating them. These may be competitive charts that contrast one child with his siblings, or they may simply be records of accomplishment. (This latter tack is better if you don't want to foster a competitive atmosphere between your kids, or if your child is, at least so far, an "only.") The six-year-old who gets a check mark for every task he accomplishes during the day and a gold star on the chart if he gets all his assigned tasks done by the end of the day is being motivated much the same way as are those office workers.

Of course, rewards fall under the heading of motivation. A reward doesn't have to be a sweet. "You can pick the movie we watch tonight" is a reward. So is "You can sit in the special place at the table," or "You get to wear the hat of honor." (The "hat of honor" can be anything from a base-ball cap with a special significance to a homemade paper crown.)

But rewards don't have to be tangible. Praise is a reward too. And the good corporate manager knows that praise is a wonderful motivator. The parent who tells her three-year-old, "Good job," when the child puts her pants on right side front is using praise effectively. (The parent who uses praise effusively for every little thing is *not* using praise effectively. It loses its currency. It ceases to have meaning. Be judicious in how often you praise and how lavishly. But don't stint needlessly. To use my own mother's favorite word: moderation. Moderation is the key.)

Employees generally enjoy pleasing their boss, and kids generally enjoy pleasing their mother, for some of the same reasons. Most of us have a respect for authority and like to know we're in favor with those above us.

If you're at the top of the corporate ladder, you know that those under you seek to impress you and win your favor, both because of the actual rewards they can reap (promotions, salary raises and bonuses, perks such as corner offices) and because most people simply like to be "in good" with the boss. If you're in the middle of the corporate ladder, you probably have peo-ple trying to curry your favor even as you do your best to impress your super-visors. And if you're low on the ladder, you're probably in a position of trying to make a good impression on your own supervisors.

In the corporate world, the old "carrot and stick" theory is very much alive and well. There are "carrots" such as perks, raises, bonuses, promotions, and other incentives to keep the employees eager to work hard in quest of rewards. There are also "sticks" such as docking an employee's pay or pro-moting one employee over another, which serve to incentivize the employee who hasn't responded to the "carrots."

It's no secret that the same carrot and stick methodology works in parent-ing too. Moms and dads have been using it for years. The "carrot" can be some-thing as simple as a smile, a kiss from Mom or Dad, or a "Good job" and a loving pat on the tush. (Of course such simple rewards are more effective with four-year-olds than fourteen-year-olds, but even fourteen-year-olds like feeling appreciated.) It can be a gold star on a chart for the child making her bed without being told to, or cleaning her room. It can be being given a privilege (or being allowed to skip a chore). It can be a treat, whether that's a hot fudge sundae, a trip to the games arcade or the zoo, or an extra story at bedtime. It can be a tangible reward: "Get all A's for two semesters and I'll buy you a new bike."

The "stick" is often a revocation of privileges: "Clean your room or no TV tonight." "If your chores aren't all taken care of on time this week, you're not getting your allowance." "If you hit your brother again, you won't be allowed to have your friend sleep over this weekend."

Empowerment is another tool that works as well at home as it does in the corporate culture. When you want your employees to do well on a particular project, you give them a certain amount of authority, of latitude, of discretion to run with the project. You allow them to make a number of key decisions within a certain scope and to be in charge—to whatever extent is suitable—of the ongoing project and its outcome.

The same tool works with the "subordinates" of your household, though different techniques, and different degrees of self-determination, are suitable at different ages. With a twelve-year-old, it might be that you tell him on a Sunday morning, "I want your room cleaned, the leaves raked, and your laundry folded by dinnertime at six o'clock. I leave it up to you to decide when to do these things. I'm not going to tell you you have to get all your chores done first. If you want to go shoot hoops with the guys first, that's okay. Just so your chores are all done by dinnertime, without fail. When you do them is up to you. You're old enough now to understand how to manage your time."

Key phrases such as "You're old enough now" and "I leave it up to you to decide" are empowering. By giving the child a degree of latitude and the power to make decisions, you leave him feeling in charge of getting his tasks done. Compare this with having the child do each task *when* you tell him, *because* you tell him. Isn't accomplishment through empowerment easier on both him and you?!

Put him in charge of his list of tasks, make him feel he's earned the right (through maturity and/or past performance) to make some of his own decisions, and watch him strive to make sure he gets to keep that right. Also watch him strive to please you—"the boss"—even if there's no further tangible benefit on offer.

Another form of empowerment is decision-making. Let's say that every fall you have each of your kids try on their last year's fall and winter clothes to see which still fit and which need to be handed down or given away. And let's say that every year the kids groan at this boring prospect, while you yourself are none too thrilled either, though you keep your groans silent.

Perhaps this year your daughter is old enough for you to tell her, "Honey, I want you to go to your room and try on all your last year's fall and winter things. You're old enough now to know what looks like it still fits and what's too tight, too short, or too overall skimpy. Please take all your fall and winter clothes out and put them on the bed. Try each one on. Look in the mirror. Then put the ones that fit back in the closet or the dresser, wherever they all belong. And leave on your bed whatever doesn't fit right anymore."

Now you've empowered your daughter with the challenge of making good decisions about her wardrobe. You, of course, can override any decision she makes. You're still "the boss." When you look through the pile of clothes on the bed, you may find something that has a hem that can be let down or a seam that can be let out. You may find some clothes that will still do for around the house, even though they're no longer in good enough shape to be worn to school or anywhere else outside the house. You can overrule any of her decisions you want to. But by empowering her with the initial decision-making responsibility, you've motivated her to undertake the task, and you've gotten yourself off the hook for that task. Now all you have to do is validate her decisions and make note of what needs to be replaced.

Yet you're not giving up your own power when you empower your kids. If you think at three o'clock that your son is at risk of not accomplishing all his tasks on time, you can prompt him, "You *are* going to have your room, the yard, and your laundry done by dinnertime, right?" If you think your daughter has cast off an item of clothing simply because she doesn't like it, you can still ask her to try it on for your appraisal. And in other situations, you can ask a question such as, "Do you need any help in budgeting your time?" or "Do you want any hints on how to best accomplish that task?" that will gently prod the kids into doing an assigned chore or help them accomplish it most effectively.

You're still the boss, and you're still in charge of the company. You're still the one who'll get praised or blamed by the world at large—and in your own mind as well—according to what kind of kids your children are, and what kind of adults and what kind of citizens of the world they grow up to be. You're still the one they need to listen to, and the one they'll want to please. You're the boss.

Now, where do you want to lead them? We'll talk about that in the next chapter.

2

WHAT IS YOUR MISSION?

The CEO of a company, large or small, has a mission, as does the company itself. In concert with her board of directors, or her managers, or her assistant—depending on the size of the company and its setup—the head of the company formulates a mission statement. *What does this company want to do, besides make money? What are the company's goals? What are its aims? And what are her personal goals within the company? What direction does she want to lead it in?*

These mission statements—both the corporate one and the CEO's own mission statement—help shape and define the direction the company is taking, and the steps the CEO is taking to get the company on the right track and keep it there. These mission statements help clarify not only the thinking of the CEO but that of the other decision-makers and policy-makers in the upper echelons of management.

Moms, too, have a mission, or a series of missions. It helps if you can clearly define yours.

Like any CEO, it helps if you have both short-range goals and long-range goals. Once you have clarified these, you can begin to work on identifying and clarifying what steps you need to take to accomplish the goals you have set for yourself.

"Raising the kids" is too broad a concept to qualify for a mission statement. Yes, of course, you want to raise the kids, but let's be a little more specific than that.

"Getting through the day without losing it" may seem to be your main mission on those days when everything goes wrong, when the toddler flushes your engagement ring down the toilet, the four-year-old exhibits his mastery of the art of the temper tantrum, your seven-year-old brings a note home from school reminding you that you need to send her to school with cupcakes for all the kids in class tomorrow (and this is the first you've heard about it!), your husband is home with the flu and demanding more attention than all three kids put together, and the dog has got diarrhea and has "redecorated" every carpet in the house. On days like that, "getting through the day without losing it" may be the only goal that seems feasible, and you have your doubts about even that goal! But while some days are like that, you really do need a better mission statement overall.

Start by defining what you want for the kids. Is it for each child to achieve his or her best potential? For your two daughters to grow up to be self-sufficient, so that they never need to be dependent on marriage for satisfaction or for financial support? Is it that you want to raise moral kids who respect their neighbors on the block and on the planet? Is it that you want to raise kids who, above all, love God? Is it that you want to raise children who will always treat Mother Earth as well as they treat their own mother? Do you want to raise your son to be manly, or to be comfortable when he's in touch with his feminine side? Or is neither of those of great importance to you? Do you want to raise your daughter to be free-spirited and independent, a postfeminist girl who takes it for granted that she will have a career and that no career path is closed to her? Or do you want to raise her to believe that motherhood is her first and most important career? Or is neither of those beliefs of great importance to you?

What are your short-term goals for your kids, *now,* and in the very short-range future? What are your long-term goals for your kids? Though you can't realistically decide that your infant is going to be a doctor or that your one-year-old is going to be a musician, you *can* decide whether you're going to try to aim your kids toward professional careers or just let them follow their own inner voices toward careers. And (more important to most parents) you can decide what values and beliefs you want to instill in them.

While you cannot be sure that your children will adopt the values you try to instill in them, you need to at least try. And so, part of formulating a mission statement involves deciding what kind of children you want to raise.

You may not succeed in raising them to be as polite, or as motivated, or as caring, or as introspective, or as extroverted as you want. To a great degree, the traits they'll exhibit and develop are dependent on the personalities they're born with, and also on the way they're shaped by the larger environment around them: their friends, schoolmates, teachers, and all the other people they'll come in contact with, as well as by the events in their lives that impact them. But you can decide which traits and values are the most important for you to try to instill or nurture in them. Assuredly your kids cannot be everything you want them to be. You need to prioritize what's the most important.

But there are other decisions you need to make, too. Your goals need to encompass more than just the values, beliefs, and character traits you want to try to bring out in your kids.

What kind of a home life do you want to offer them? Are you going to be the kind of mother who dedicates her life to her kids and is always at their beck and call? Or do you have other priorities of your own? There's no shame in that. It certainly provides a good example for them, if you want them to grow up to be independent individuals with fulfilling lives! And if you totally give up a career you love in order to become a stay-at-home mom "for the kids" and wind up resenting them (an all-too-human reaction), you're not doing them any favor!

Are you going to try to run a business from home? Or take a job that can largely be performed as a telecommuter working from home? Are you going to lead by example and show the kids that being a well-rounded person involves having interests outside the family? Or are you going to, still leading by example, show the kids that family is the most important thing in your life? Perhaps you have no choice but to work outside the home, and rather than grumbling about it, you'll use it as an object lesson to show the kids that even grown-ups don't always get to do what they want, and that sometimes we have to do what we have to do, whether or not we like it. They can learn from your example to deal with reality and make the best of it. The way you prioritize your life, whether of necessity or by choice, can be a great lesson for your kids. So part of defining your goals and your mission statement is deciding what lessons you want your lifestyle to teach your kids.

If you aren't a single mom (divorced, widowed, or never married), raising the kids alone, then you have a husband, and part of your figuring out your mission statement is likely to involve him. Not only do you probably have a goal or mission in regard to your marriage, separate from what you want for your kids, but your goals for the kids involve at least some help, cooperation, and input from your husband or significant other. Once you've formulated a set of goals and a mission statement for raising the kids, you'd better make sure your parenting partner is on the same page.

Your partner may have a different set of goals in mind for the kids than you do. And that's usually all right, the exception being when your goals and his are mutually exclusive. Fortunately that doesn't happen very often. Usually it's a matter of differing priorities. You think that the most important thing of all is to raise kids who are fulfilled and happy. He thinks the most important thing of all is to raise kids who are financially independent. Neither of you disagrees that the other's goal is important; you just each feel that your own goal is more important. As long as the two goals don't clash, there's no real problem.

All right—what do you need to actually *do* now?

First, find a quiet time and place. (That may be the hardest part of all, but there really are such moments of sanity in every mother's life, even if they occur only between 10:00 p.m., when the thirteen-year-old goes to bed, and 1:00 a.m., when the baby wakes up for his feeding.) Now sit down with a paper and pen (or at your computer) and *think*. Think about what your goals are for your kids, both short-range and long-range. Next, go over those goals and choose the most important ones. Mark them with asterisks, or number the list in order of importance, or use yellow highlighter—whatever system works for you.

Next think what your goals are for the family overall, as a unit. (Now you are probably thinking medium-range, rather than short-term or long-term.) Again, prioritize these goals. Which are the most important to you?

There are no "right answers" or "wrong answers," as long as they're *true answers* and *your answers*. These should not be what your mother would want for the family, or what your Aunt Fanny always said (unless you agree with what your aunt espoused), or what some magazine or another says is important or should be your goal. There are no "should-be's" here. You must be true to yourself. *What is important to you? What do you want for your family?*

Once you have defined these goals, both for the kids and for the family as a unit, and once you have prioritized them, you know what you're working for. You're not simply trying to raise a family, and you're not just trying to get through from day to day without a meltdown. *You have definite goals in mind.*

Now formulate a mission statement: What is your mission? What do you need to do to bring about the goals you have in mind for your kids and for your family overall?

With your mission in mind and your goals in mind, you now have your sights on a target. Like a good CEO, you've identified what it is you want to accomplish, rather than simply getting by from day to day. Whether your most important goal is to raise intelligent, educated kids, or to raise courteous, considerate kids, or to raise independent kids—or if your goal is something else altogether—you're working toward a specific goal now.

It should come as no surprise that the next thing you need to do is decide what steps you need to take to accomplish each of these goals you've defined as most important: the one or several goals you want to help your children achieve, and the one or several goals you've set for your family. Having a mission statement is a fine thing, but of course an effective CEO knows that it takes work to meet goals, work not only on the part of the employees of the corporation but also work on the part of the executives.

So decide what it is that you need to do, decide what help you need from your husband, and decide what you need the kids to do as well.

If your goal is to make sure that each child discovers her talents and makes the best use of them, what do you (and your husband) need to do to help each child learn where her talents lie? How do you encourage her to develop her talents and practice them? And what does the child need to do to nurture and hone her talents?

If your goal is to raise courteous, considerate, and thoughtful children, what do you (and your husband) need to do to instill and foster these traits in your kids? How do you encourage the kids to be the kind of people you want them to be? How do you most effectively discourage them from behaving otherwise? How should you react when one of them is thoughtless or inconsiderate?

If your goal for your family is to promote family unity and family loyalty, what do you (and your husband) need to do to encourage family unity and family harmony in the kids—and in yourselves? What attitudes on your part, what activities on the family's part, will foster these feelings in the kids and in all of you? What do you need to teach the kids or show the kids that will help bring about the attitudes you're trying to encourage? What stories of family history can you tell the kids that will exemplify the attributes you're trying to engender in the children? How do you need to adjust your own behavior to be a better example?

Always keep your eyes on the target, and map out the road by which you mean to reach it. Your mission statement is the start. And, like any effective CEO, be prepared to alter your tactics if you find that you're not meeting your goals. Sometimes, yes, it's necessary to modify or change your goals, but more often what you need to change is your methods.

You're not just trying to raise kids, or to get through another day. You have goals. You want to accomplish something. Know what it is. And then work toward it.

Here is a brief, simple, and succinct sample corporate mission statement: "Acme Frammis sells and services budget-priced frammises with some of the features found on more expensive frammises and with no compromise in quality despite the low cost, stands behind its product with reliable service, and aims to be known as the affordable frammis company with products that don't sacrifice quality."

Your mission statement can be just as brief, or it can be longer. Here is a sample succinct mission statement from a mother: "Donna Ipsnagle is a caring, committed mother whose most important goal is to raise children who respect other people's points of view and ways of life, and who honor their family members first and all their fellow humans as well, in addition to respecting God and our planet Earth."

As you can see, a mission statement does not encompass all your goals and all your aspirations but rather distills the essence of what you are trying to accomplish and the endeavors you feel are supremely important. There may be many things you wish to teach your children that fall under the heading of "respect other people's points of view and ways of life" or "honor their family members . . . and . . . their fellow humans" and "respect God and . . . Earth." But these statements best distill what you have in mind overall.

Make a list of the goals you have as a mother. What do you most want to teach your kids? What values do you most want to instill in your kids? What do you most want to accomplish as a mother? Now try to find one predominant theme in all this: learning respect, learning to think for oneself, learning obedience, honoring the family, learning to serve one's fellow human beings, making the best of one's own potential—these are some examples. Is there one overarching goal that encompasses all or most of the life lessons you want to impart to your kids, or most of what you want to do for your kids? If you can't reduce it to just one, can you reduce your goals to no more than three?

Now write your own mission statement. Here's a little help in case you're at a bit of a loss:

What are your goals for your kids and for the family overall? I'm not referring here to your career goals for your kids; you may want Jonny to grow up to be a doctor, but if Jonny is squeamish at the sight of blood or simply has no interest in medicine, all your wishes and plans in the world aren't going to turn him into a doctor. (And in the extremely unlikely event that he becomes one to please you, he's going to be one unhappy physician—which surely isn't what you want!)

But if Sheila has a gift for singing or playing the violin, your long-range plans for her might include the fact that she will be trained in singing over the next few years, so that whether she becomes a rock singer, an opera singer, or someone who sings in television commercials, she can put her voice to use professionally *if she wants,* and if not, she'll be good enough to be the church choir soloist *if she chooses to,* and if not, she'll be able to sing for her friends at social gatherings *if she pleases.* The point is not to plan her career but to plan to develop her innate talent and, once she's had her voice trained, let her do with it as she pleases.

So a part of your mission statement might be to help Sheila develop her vocal talent so that she can do whatever she wants with her gift and do it well.

But a mission statement for a mom isn't only about her kids' talents. What are your goals in mothering? What is it you want to imbue in your kids?

Some part of the list below might coincide with some of your mission statement. *Please don't be overwhelmed. No one is suggesting that all these items need to be part of your mission statement, or indeed that any of them need to be.* This is merely to help you get thinking, in case all you can think of is "to be the best mother I can and help the kids grow up to be good people."

- To help the kids develop their innate skills and talents and gifts.
- To teach them not just good manners, but the genuine concern for other people and their feelings that good manners are really all about.
- To imbue them with respect for our Earth, teach them the "green" way of living, and raise them to not just recycle but be proactive in preserving our planet.
- To have them become involved in at least one social or charitable cause and work for it.
- To teach them the meaning of true charity and to be sure they learn the good feelings that come from not just giving money but giving time, giving of yourself for a good cause.
- To teach them that true charity goes beyond just giving time or money to worthy causes but also involves being charitable to individuals who may need their time, their caring, or their help.
- To teach them not to judge others too quickly but to remember the old Native American saying about not judging another man

till you have walked a mile in his moccasins, and to truly live by that precept.

- To teach them not to gossip, not to spread any story till they are positive it is true, and, even then, to ask themselves: What is to be gained by repeating this story? Who will be hurt if I repeat it? And if in doubt, to keep their mouths shut.
- To teach them to have respect for other people's differences and not look down on others who are not like them, whether the difference is in temperament, in background, in intelligence, or in physical ability.
- To teach them to get involved in politics, at minimum to vote. Regardless of which party they affiliate with or which candidate they vote for, the important thing is to not take our democracy for granted nor to complain about the way the country is being run if they didn't take steps to get the best possible candidates elected.
- To teach them to take pride in whatever they do, whether it's an occupation or a hobby or a necessary task that they view as drudgery. To teach them to do their best at all they do, and not to slough off a task or chore simply because it's boring or unsatisfying.
- To teach them to respect the rights and the property of others.
- To teach them honesty, honor, and integrity. To teach them not only not to lie but to always conduct themselves with the highest degree of honor and integrity in all matters.
- To teach them to be open to new experiences of all sorts and yet cautious that they not try anything dangerous or foolhardy or illegal.
- To teach them to respect the laws of the land and of their own state and municipality even if they don't agree with them.
- To teach them the American way of working for change when they have a quarrel with the laws or workings of the government.
- To teach them to have a good work ethic and give one hundred percent of their effort and energy to any project, whether in their professional or personal lives.
- To teach them to be accepting of other people's backgrounds, whether ethnic, economic, or otherwise, when others are different from them.
- To teach them to respect their own bodies by eating right, getting enough exercise, and not ingesting substances that are bad for them, including cigarettes and drugs as well as excessive junk foods.
- To teach them to love God and pray to Him, and not just when they want to ask Him for something.

- To teach them to love and respect their family and remember that allegiance to family members comes ahead of allegiance to any friends.
- To teach them patience and tolerance with other people's faults and foibles.
- To teach them to respect the value of friendship, and to always remember that to have a good friend, one must be a good friend.
- To teach them the necessary skills for independent living, such as cooking and housekeeping, whether they are boys or girls.
- To teach them that if a thing is worth doing, it is worth doing right.
- To instill in them a love of learning.
- To help them become eager to try new things and new experiences, rather than being nervous about or reluctant about the unexplored.
- To instill in them a genuine desire to be helpful to others.
- To teach them to deal straightforwardly in their relationships with others and not "play games."
- To teach them that the two sexes are different but equal, that there *are* differences between men and women but that those differences do not make either sex better than the other. To teach them that all career possibilities are applicable to both men and women, an important lesson to boys as well as girls, since a boy may one day grow up to be an employer or grow up to want a job in a field formerly thought of as "women's work."
- To teach them to take pride in all they do and be proud of who and what they are as well.
- To teach them to always try to improve themselves and correct their faults, yet not to be hard on themselves for their lack of perfection, since *nobody* is perfect.

These are some of the qualities and teachings you may strive for in your mission statement for the kids. You may have others you wish to include—by no means is this a complete list, or everyone's list. The point is for you to *have* a list, whether it's written or whether it's simply in your head.

What else might be part of your mission statement? What else do you want for your family?

Some of your mission statement will include things for *you* to do. Again, these are only suggestions, and you do not need to include them all, or include any of them. They are merely ideas:

- Be sure the kids hear ample praise from your lips and not just criticisms or corrections of their actions.
- Be sure the kids know they are loved and valued.
- Be sure you display a good example for the kids, so that your behavior around them is not a case of "Do as I say, not as I do."
- Be loving with your husband, and be sure that you and he show each other respect, consideration, and affection, so that the kids have good role models for their future relationships.
- If you are divorced, be respectful of your ex and don't degrade him to your children, no matter what you really think of him. Save your gripes for your friends, and speak of him decently and honorably in front of the kids.
- Be respectful and considerate of your own parents, so that you set a good example for the kids. If either of your parents is difficult to be with, save your complaints for your friends or your husband, out of earshot of the kids.
- Don't be mistrustful or suspicious of what the kids tell you unless you have due cause or provocation.
- Trust the kids (within limits of what's appropriate to their ages) unless and until they give you a reason not to trust them.
- Respect your own body and take good care of it, both so that the kids have a good example to follow and so that you stay in good condition for taking care of them.
- Don't be afraid to say, "I messed up," when you did. It teaches the kids to be willing to admit to their own mistakes.
- When you do mess up, try to do better next time, and to make amends this time if your mistake was one that caused pain or discomfort or damage to someone else.
- Don't lie to the kids. (Santa and tooth fairy stories don't count as lies!)
- Don't favor one child over the other in your words, your actions, or your attitude, no matter what you feel in your heart.
- Exercise patience with the kids, even if you're having a bad day. If you do lose your temper, apologize. (That will set a good example.)
- Teach them the value of money and how to save it. Also try to instill in them a willingness to earn, so that they don't expect you to hand them money every time they want something. This way they won't grow up expecting the world to hand them their wants on the proverbial silver platter.

- Try to instill in them a love of reading. Start by reading to them often when they're little.
- Don't ever try to "buy" their love—either with toys or other gifts, or by spoiling them in other ways. And if you've been less available to them than you'd like to be, whether because you've had to work late or for whatever other reason, don't give them material things out of guilt or as a "make-nice" for your unavailability.
- When you fail at one of these precepts, or in some other way you're not the sort of mother you'd like to be, remember that you are only human and no one succeeds one hundred percent of the time. Just resolve to try harder, but don't berate yourself. Making a better effort is constructive; mentally beating yourself up is not.
- Teach your children to respect those in authority, but if you ever think such a person (for example a teacher or scoutmaster) is abusing his authority or abusing your child's trust, or simply being unfair, step in and protect your child, or at least investigate to learn what's really happening.

Your mission statement might also include such items as:

- I want to make sure that the kids know not just their immediate family but their extended family.
- I want the kids to know as much as possible about their family heritage, national heritage, religious heritage, and cultural heritage.
- I want to give the kids as many cultural experiences as is practical and financially feasible.
- I want to expose the kids to as many life experiences as is reasonable.
- I want the kids to see as many parts of the country, or the world, as is practical and affordable.
- I want the kids to see urban, rural, and suburban areas, regardless of which we live in ourselves.

Other possible goals or decisions might include:

- I want the kids to work to pay for at least part of their college tuition even if we can afford to pay it all, because an education they've paid for themselves, or at least helped pay for, by their own labor will be more meaningful to them.

- I want the kids to grow up to be as well-rounded as possible.
- I will not try to mold the kids in my image, nor will I try to force them to be interested in what I'd like them to be interested in. I will respect their individuality and their personalities and their interests.
- I will expose the kids to as many industries and workplaces as is realistically feasible to help them be more aware of the array of careers and industries that exist for them to choose from.
- I will always remember to be sure the kids know that I love them, even when I am displeased with something they have done or am in disagreement with some of their thinking.

Above all, decide what is most important to you in raising your kids—what values, what goals, what experiences you want them to have. Then set yourself a road map for achieving these ideals. What doesn't make it into your mission statement might still be part of an adjunct list.

Discuss these decisions, your goals and your mission statement, with your husband. Make sure you are not working at cross-purposes with each other.

Review your lists (whether written or mental), your goals, and your decisions periodically. There may be an item or two you want to add. There may be a mid-course correction you want to issue yourself as to how to achieve your objectives. You may just need a periodic reminder of what it is you wish to accomplish. In the day-to-day reality of raising kids, and of carrying on with the rest of your life at the same time (being a wife, a daughter to your parents, a friend to your friends, and quite possibly balancing a career with all this too), it's easy to lose sight of your goals and wishes. Sometimes it's all you can do to make sure Jan has clean socks and panties for school tomorrow and Pete has his homework finished, without finding time to imbue them with culture or with an appreciation for the diversity of the world. Sometimes teaching them to wipe and flush seems so beyond what's possible that teaching them understanding or teaching them to respect other people's property seems totally out of the question.

But even when you have to abandon your objectives for the moment, to deal with the exigencies of day-to-day living, remember that a good executive keeps her eyes on the larger goal even as she deals with the smaller and more immediate ones. And the smaller goals *are part of what you need in order to accomplish the larger goals in your mission statement.* So keep your eyes on the larger goals and the smaller ones, both, and forge ahead.

3

WHICH HAT ARE
YOU WEARING?

Carlie is a typical mom. On a not particularly unusual Thursday morning, her alarm clock wakes her up half an hour earlier than she usually sets it for, and for a fuzzy moment or two she wonders why it malfunctioned. Then she remembers that she staggered off to bed the night before too exhausted to do anything more, but without finishing helping her son with his diorama, which is due in school today. What's more, she has to drop off the dog at the groomer's this morning, before she puts her nine-year-old on the school bus, takes the three-year-old to day care, and goes to work.

Before all that, of course, she has to get herself dressed, get the three-year-old dressed, make breakfast for everyone, make lunches for the two kids, and do a quick check on dinner to be sure the necessary ingredients are in place, and no ravenous family member has mistaken any of them for an available snack, and that the lettuce for the salad hasn't wilted overnight beyond usability.

On her way through the kitchen she glances at the bulletin board and realizes that the coupon tacked up there that was good for a free oil change expired yesterday unused, although the van is certainly overdue for an oil change, with all the miles she's been putting on it. As her gaze shifts downward, she observes that an army of ants is performing maneuvers on her countertop (again!) and stops to write a note to call the exterminator. (The visit will be free under the service contract; it's finding a mutually convenient *time* to schedule him that's the problem!)

Carlie's husband comes into the kitchen now, looking for a cup of coffee. Carlie hasn't started the coffee yet. Hubby sighs but goes to the sink and fills the carafe, pitching in but grumbling that he has an early meeting and is pressed for time, "And I can't find my blue dress shirt." Carlie remembers that laundry was one of the things she'd meant to get to last night but never found the time for before giving up, exhausted, and heading to bed. The shirt in question is still reposing in the laundry basket.

The three-year-old makes his first appearance of the day, standing in the kitchen naked from the waist down. Carlie is grateful that she won't have to wake him up this morning, but her gratitude is short-lived. "Mommmmm. My bed is wet."

More laundry, and she'd better add a quick bath for her younger son to the growing list of tasks that need to be accomplished this morning.

The phone rings. It's one of her fellow managers from the office. "I hate to bother you so early, but I came to work very early, and the donut shop wasn't even open yet. Can you bring the donuts and muffins for the meeting?"

"Mom! There's no juice! What am I supposed to drink? What am I supposed to bring to school?" It's the voice of her nine-year-old. "Don't forget you have to take me to band practice after school," he adds.

"I can't! Big work project—I can't leave early. Isn't Dana's mom taking you?"

"That was last week. It's your turn."

Carlie turns to her husband. "Can you grab this one?"

"I have to see what I've got going at work. I'll call you at the office later."

The nine-year-old pipes up again. "Who's gonna take me?" he wails.

Now it's the three-year-old's turn: "Sparky needs to go out. He's scratching the door."

Carlie turns to the nine-year-old. "Can you take him, honey?"

"What about my diorama?"

What about a little sanity?

What about better time management?

Both in your work life and in your home life, you're probably used to budgeting your money. At work, you might be in charge of the entire company or of one department, but either way you know you have a set amount of money to work with and have to make it stretch to cover all needs and contingencies. At the beginning of the year, or the fiscal year, or the quarter, or the month (or all of these, by turns), you sit down and take a look at what monies you have at your disposal and what expenditures you anticipate having to make. You balance your availabilities with your needs and contingencies, and you come up with a workable plan for the period in question.

Like all plans, it may well need to be changed as situations arise unexpectedly, whether it's a shortfall of income or an unexpected expenditure. Budgets often need to be adjusted; seldom are they set in stone.

In your home life, too, you're probably used to budgeting your money. You know that, absent the unexpected, you can anticipate having such-and-such an amount of income each month to work with, and you can also anticipate certain expenses. Your electric bill is likely to be so much, your food expenses so much, your mortgage or rent so much, and so on. If nothing intervenes to throw your budget off kilter, you'll make it through the month without a problem.

If your daughter breaks her arm and winds up in the E.R., of course that's going to throw your budget out of whack. Depending on your circumstances, that may mean raiding the savings account, cashing in some stocks, calling a creditor to explain why your payment is going to be late, asking your well-off sister for a loan, selling on eBay a few rare books from your collection, or canceling the family trip to Disney World. But even before Lisa falls off her skateboard, you know in the back of your head what your options would be in such a circumstance, because, as a good money manager, you've thought ahead to what you would do were there to be a sudden emergency that overtaxed your budget.

Do you budget your time as well as you budget your money?

Probably not. The average mom doesn't.

Of course, no matter how well you budget your time, emergencies and other last-minute circumstances are bound to pop up. When your daughter falls off her skateboard, breaks her arm, and has to be rushed to the E.R., it impacts not only your financial budget but your time budget. What did you expect to be doing during the time you now will spend sitting in the E.R. waiting room? Whether it was patching the knees of that same daughter's jeans, or checking over your son's homework, or cooking dinner, or baking a cake for your husband's birthday, or spending fifteen minutes de-stressing with a good book, suddenly your whole time budget has gone to hell in the proverbial handbasket.

Of course, not all time-thieves are as dramatic as a broken arm. If your daughter needs more help than usual with her homework, or needs your help with writing a poem for her after-school club, or asks you to please let her start planning her birthday party (which requires your input), that's a much less dramatic situation, but still one that requires time you hadn't planned on spending. If the meat you took out of the freezer last night hasn't defrosted in the fridge as it should have, if your son comes home from Scouts with a new badge he wants sewn onto his uniform right away (and you choose to honor the request), if he calls from school and asks if he may please bring Adam home with him and can Adam stay for dinner (which requires augmenting the menu), if the cat decides that *now* is the time to have her kittens (with the whole family watching, of course!), or if your best friend calls and says, "Quick! Turn on Channel 4! Susie's going to be on the six o'clock news!" your well-budgeted time is going to suddenly run short.

The best-laid plans "gang aft agley," and the best-planned time can similarly be thrown askew. No matter how well you budget your time, something's going to throw that old monkey wrench into the works on occasion. But with a reasonable amount of planning, you can handle most day-to-day situations without being knocked for a loop or thrown into a tizzy, and you'll even be better able to handle the situations that do come up and wreak havoc with your schedule from time to time.

What am I talking about? *Not* anything as compulsive as planning your time down to the minute. I am not recommending that you go to the extreme of planning your mornings and your evenings (and your days, if you've left the business world for now and are staying at home to raise the kids) second by second. I think writing "7:03—Shower" is more than a little extreme.

But chances are you have a Things to Do list (or possibly even more than one—perhaps one for things that need doing in general and one for things specifically to do today). This is the beginning of a time budget. Now let's refine it even more.

I use my computer to compile a Things to Do list every morning. Of course you can write yours by hand if you wish, but using the computer saves you from rewriting when you make your new day's list—all those items that didn't get accomplished and crossed off yesterday, either because you ran short of time or, more likely, because they were items you didn't expect to get to till some day later on.

To better budget your time, don't just list what needs to be done; list when you intend to do it. Again, I don't mean for you to plan down to the minute, but you can group the items on your list so that you know what you have to do before you leave for work, or before you wake the kids up, or according to whatever your particular time delineators are.

If you need to leave work early to get Rob at Scouts, or you need to stop on the way to work and pick up paper towels or printer ink, or you need to drop off some library books on your lunch hour or pick up a present for your daughter's friend's birthday party, write it on the list in the appropriate place. This will allow you to plan better, to better budget your time, and to see more clearly which tasks can be accomplished at the same time as others (for example, ironing while a cake is in the oven) or on the same errand as others.

You already know you have certain regular tasks to accomplish every day, and you know roughly how much time each of these tasks accounts for. You probably won't want to list these. It probably isn't necessary to write down "Make Allison's lunch" (unless she normally eats the school lunch and today, or tomorrow, is going to be an exception). Similarly, if you pick Scott up at school every day, you don't need to list that, but if he normally takes the bus and tomorrow you need to pick him up for some reason, then you'll need to list it. But does a regular item—say, "Cook dinner"—have an unusual aspect to it tomorrow? Are you using your slow cooker tomorrow? And do you therefore need to remember to get dinner going before you leave the house for work in the morning? Or are you cooking something on the stove or in the oven that has to be started several hours earlier than usual or has to start marinating in the morning? You're a stay-at-home mom who usually gets dinner started around five o'clock, but tomorrow do you need to remember to start cooking at three, or to prepare a marinade and put the pork tenderloin in it before you go off to work? Under these circumstances, put "Dinner up at three" or "Dinner in slow cooker" or "Marinate pork" on your list.

Now that you've written all necessary items on your Things to Do list, look at your list and see where each of the items you need to get done will best fit into your schedule. Will you have time to call the plumber before you leave for work? Write it down in the Before Work section of your list. If his office isn't open yet at that hour, can you call him from work? If that won't work, how about calling him from your van, using your cell phone, after you drop Jeremy off at day care? You need to bring cookies to the Scout meeting tomorrow. They don't need to be homemade; store-bought will do fine. But you don't have enough cookies in the house. You can buy them quickly at the convenience store, at convenience store prices. Or you can save money by buying them at the supermarket, which means an extra trip, with the inherent time needed for finding parking, navigating the aisles, standing in line, and checking out. But—aha!—you're planning ahead now. What if you did all your grocery shopping tonight, instead of Friday night? You could pick up the cookies along with everything else you need, and you'd buy back some time for Friday's schedule. What else do you have to do tonight? Is getting your groceries for the week doable then? Now you're really budgeting your time!

The van is due in for minor service. The auto shop is only a quarter of a mile from Jon's pediatrician, and Jon has an appointment to get his pre-camp physical next Tuesday. You could make an appointment to bring the van in right after Jon's appointment. That would save some time. And if the work on the van is something to be done while you wait, what can you bring with you to work on in the waiting room? You can make sure Jon brings his homework, and you bring a project too. Sure, they have good magazines and a TV in the waiting room, but ignore all that and be productive. Plan the week's menus, or bring along your sewing, or bring that stack of newspaper inserts from which you've been meaning to clip coupons, or . . . well, you know what's on your Things to Do list. Which of the items is easily portable and can be accomplished while you wait for the van to be serviced?

Budget your time. Plan ahead. Don't make five separate errand runs in the same general direction if you can accomplish it all in one or two runs. Don't make extra trips to the supermarket if it's avoidable. Don't sit at the hair salon or in the dentist's waiting room unproductively *killing time* when you could be helping yourself by *filling time* accomplishing something.

And what if the time you need to fill catches you without a project at hand, or it's simply not convenient to pull out your knitting, or to carry around the photo album and the pictures you need to put into it? Don't forget that *thinking* is accomplishing something, too. Those minutes while the dentist is drilling or the hairstylist is cutting, those times when you're stuck in traffic or waiting at the airport for a delayed incoming flight are all prime thinking and planning time. Not, of course, if you're keeping one eye on a hyperactive four-year-old, or even if you're having to answer the questions of a restless or inquisitive nine-year-old. But if you're alone, or if your child is safely occupied, turn those otherwise idle moments to productive use.

Plan menus, plan your next vacation, plan what you're going to do with that leftover fabric, plan which of Jennifer's friends she might spend the night with next Friday while you and your husband go to that dinner party, plan how you're going to celebrate Eric's next birthday. Think about what you're going to get your parents for their upcoming anniversary. Formulate an answer to be ready with the next time Brian says, "But the other kids say there is no Santa Claus," or "But how did the baby get *into* your tummy?"

Always carry a small-size spiral notepad with you. (Find it at the office supply store.) Use it to make notes of things you think of to add to your

Things to Do list, to write down menus you plan in those odd moments you'd rather fill productively than waste, to write down that question for Gina's teacher that occurred to you at the last red light, to jot down any ideas you have at all.

And consider carrying a small cassette recorder in the car with you. Yes, I know—your car, van, or SUV has a built-in CD or tape recorder for playing music. What I'm suggesting is that you carry a tape recorder with blank or reusable tapes for the purpose of dictating. It's a hell of a lot easier (and safer!) to dictate into a tape recorder while you drive than to try to write and drive simultaneously. And waiting for the next red light in order to write safely isn't always effective. You might forget your ideas before then, particularly if you have two rug rats fighting in the backseat. Or if you're driving on the interstate at the moment.

Do you have two kids in the backseat? How about putting your driving time to use by drilling them in spelling words, capitals of the states, or other knowledge appropriate to their ages? It will not only be a very helpful, useful exercise, but it will break up the chorus of "He hit me first!" If these are three- and four-year-olds, sing the alphabet song with them, or help them with counting skills.

Of course not all the valuable things to do with kids involve skills drills. Questions of the "What did you do in school today?" sort work well while you're both confined in the car. (This is also an opportunity to ask your kids, "Is there anything *you* want to ask *me*?") And a little lighter mental exercise is good for the kids as well. I'm thinking now of imagination-stretchers, questions like "If you could be anyone in the world, who would you be?" "If you could have any three wishes, what would they be?" "Who do you most admire? And why?" A child's creativity is like a muscle; it benefits from being exercised and stretched. So ask imagination-stretching questions, or challenge your kids to make up stories.

In the corporate world, planning menus while you're waiting at the airport or drilling kids on skills while you're driving is called "multitasking," of course. And while we're talking about multitasking, what do you do while you're engaged in such mindless chores as doing the dishes, mopping the floors, or washing the clothes? These, too, are good times for thinking or planning. Or for giving your kids math drills or morals scenarios. ("What would you do if your best friend asked you to pass him the answers to a test?")

When I was a child, it was my chore to dry the dishes as my mother was washing them. (We didn't have a dishwasher.) Some nights, we had mother-daughter chats. (It was a chance to bond, a chance for me to ask her questions and for her to ask me questions, too.) Some nights, we sang together. (Neither of us could do better than to barely carry a tune, but that never stopped us, and the warm feelings and memories those sing-alongs engendered are something I treasure to this day.) And many evenings, as we did the dishes, we played Geography. (My mother also deemed Geography suitable for car rides. It was not only educational; it kept me from getting quite as fidgety quite as quickly.)

My mom had never heard of the term "multitasking," but that didn't stop her from being innately good at it. My mother was a good organizer, a woman who "wore many hats" comfortably and shifted seamlessly from one task to another, or juggled several at once.

Being a good CEO of your family, like being an effective CEO of any size business, means you can't sit back and simply give orders. You must be not only knowledgeable but proactively involved in many areas of your "job." You need to be able to supervise, delegate, and organize, but you also need to roll up your sleeves and get to work yourself.

On the other hand, you can't do everything yourself, either. As the kids grow into the ability to handle more and more tasks, you need to be able to delegate. And you need the patience to let them make mistakes and learn from them, perhaps with gentle guidance from you, but *not* with you saying, "Let me do it myself. That will be faster," or "That will be easier."

But having all that work to do and to supervise requires your budgeting your time wisely, and it requires your being facile at multitasking. Your "job" calls for you to be by turns chief executive and cleanup janitor, nurse and cook and dishwasher, teacher of everything from morals to manners to math, chauffeur and laundress, referee and mediator, cheerleader and coach.

And when I say "coach," I include everything from skill-coaching a toddler who's learning to walk to morals-coaching the child whom you observed shoplifting when you took him to the candy store—not to mention soccer-coaching, tetherball-coaching, and teaching how to tie a shoelace or how to wash a dog. You must learn to budget your time. You must learn to multitask. All executives must learn to, and that includes moms who are parenting in the CEO mold.

4

SELF-CONFIDENCE
IS KEY

A good executive projects self-confidence. This is then transmitted to her "troops." In an office, the chief executive must always project a certainty of direction and a certainty in herself. She can hardly expect her staff to follow her lead or to give their all if they don't believe she knows where she's going, what she's doing, what her goals and aims are, and how she's going to achieve them. And, above all, they must believe in her leadership qualities in order to be an effective team.

The same is true of Mom as the executive officer of her family. To be a good leader, you must believe in yourself. This doesn't mean believing that you're totally infallible, to the point of rigidity. If you make a rule, issue an edict, or come to a decision, and then realize that you were wrong, or simply that there's a better way, you need to correct yourself. Self-confidence is not the same thing as believing that you're always right.

Let's take an example. If your two kids are fighting, and Samantha blames Barry while Barry blames Samantha, you will need to intercede. In all probability you'll handle them both equally, whether that means simply talking to them about getting along or whether it means issuing a time-out for both. But suppose you decide that Barry was clearly to blame for starting this brouhaha, and you send him to his room while merely giving Samantha a mild reprimand. Now suppose later on you come to realize that Samantha was, in fact, the instigator, and Barry was far less to blame than you had thought. Believing in yourself does not mean believing that everything you say is always right. You need to rectify the injustice you created. To you, it may be a small matter, but of course to Samantha and, especially, to Barry, it's a matter of huge importance. It will also help instill confidence in your leadership in your kids. They will have greater respect for your leadership.

Let's take another example. Your son, age ten, wants to see a particular movie. You suspect it's not appropriate for him, and you tell him you won't allow it. Later, in talking to a friend who has seen the movie, and whose judgment you trust, you learn more about it and are persuaded that, after all, it would be okay for your son to go see that movie. Again, self-confidence does not mean believing that everything you say or do is always right. In fact, it takes self-confidence to admit you were wrong about something—in this case, the suitability of the movie. You go back to your son and say, "I've reconsidered. You may see that movie."

Do you think that makes you sound wishy-washy? Not at all. It makes you sound fair. You don't change your mind at the drop of a hat on every issue. But when you're wrong, you have enough self-confidence to admit it.

What a wonderful object lesson for your kids!

Self-confidence, you see, does not mean thinking you're always right. To the contrary, it means having enough faith in yourself that you can admit it when a decision of yours may not have been the best one, or when further facts have enlightened your thinking and made you change your mind.

But what if you don't have enough self-confidence? What if you're insecure about being a mother, either because this is your first child, or simply because you're not a very confident person overall?

Fake it.

You heard me. Fake it, and eventually you'll not only fool your kids but also fool yourself. (Remember in the classic movie *The King and I*, when Anna explains to her son that she whistles a happy tune to fool the people she fears and to fool herself as well?) If you *project* self-confidence, if you *act as if you have* self-confidence, eventually you'll *feel* self-confidence.

And till you do, you'll have the kids believing in your self-confidence even before it's real.

Kids can sense when a parent isn't sure of herself, and they know that such a parent, lacking in belief in herself, can be a pushover. If you want your kids to follow your leadership and not run roughshod over you, you need to have them believing in you and your leadership qualities. And for that to happen, you need to believe in yourself, or at least to make it appear that you do.

What are the factors that work against a mom's believing in herself?

- If it's her first child, she may be insecure in her parenting abilities.
- If she's an insecure person overall, she'll likely doubt her abilities to parent.
- If her mom did a poor job of parenting her, she may question her own ability to do any better.
- Conversely, if her mom was a supermom, she may feel she'll never be able to measure up, and she may mentally throw up her hands in despair.
- If her husband has vastly different ideas of child-raising and works against her rather than with her, or simply isn't supportive, it can undermine her self-confidence.
- If anyone close to her (such as a sister or best friend) belittles her parenting abilities constantly, it's likely to erode her self-confidence to some degree.

How do you counteract your self-doubts, other than by faking self-confidence till it's no longer an act and you believe it?

First of all, take stock of the parenting experience you do have:

- Did you have any younger siblings whom you helped take care of, or watch out for, when you were a kid? That was parenting practice!
- Did you ever babysit when you were a kid? That was parenting practice, too!
- Was your mother a good parent? Rather than feeling daunted by her expertise and feeling you can never measure up, take a lesson from her parenting skills and know that you're ahead of the game because you had such a good teacher. Even if you *don't* measure up to your own mom, think how far ahead of most *other* mothers you are. Not every mom has the benefit you do of being able to emulate such a wonderful mother as you had. Learn from her example—and outshine most other mothers.
- Was your mother a less than wonderful parent? You can still learn from her mistakes and resolve not to commit the same ones. (*Every* mother makes *some* mistakes, but at least you won't make the same

ones your own mother did. You can profit by her example in avoiding the same parenting flaws you saw in her.)

Try for just three attributes at first: firmness, fairness, and caring. By "firmness" I don't mean "strictness." Some CEOs rule with an iron hand, while others give their organizations much latitude, and the same can be said for moms. We'll discuss various parenting styles later in this book, but for now, what I want you to concentrate on is sticking to your guns unless you honestly believe you made a wrong decision.

As I said earlier, a mom with sufficient self-confidence is able to change course, admit she may have been wrong, and countermand her own orders. But that is not the same as letting your child bluff you, bluster you, hound you, or pester you into changing an edict when you know you were right in the first place.

If you honestly believe you erred in judgment, it's fine to say, "I may have been wrong. I'm going to let you start staying up half an hour later." But if Seth wants a later bedtime and you know he needs to keep going to bed at 8:00 as he does now, do not let him get you to change your mind through whining, or through telling you that all his friends stay up till 9:00, or through calling you a mean mom or telling you he won't love you anymore, or through any other tactic. Stick to what you know is right.

That's what I mean by firmness.

Fairness is a broad category but one that doesn't need much defining. It encompasses everything from not making promises you know you can't keep to not favoring one child over another. Of course there are times when you'll have to give more attention to one child than another, and of course the older child is going to have more privileges than the younger one. But don't consistently pay more attention to one child than to the other, or hand out privileges unfairly; privileges should be age-appropriate or merit-related.

And don't make promises you know you can't follow through on, or tell a child that if he does all his chores for two weeks without being reminded, you'll consider giving him a raise in his allowance, unless you really are willing to consider granting him that raise. To do otherwise isn't very fair.

Conversely, don't punish unfairly. Don't punish where it isn't warranted, and don't punish one child more sternly than the other, unless he really misbehaves that much more. Two children who commit the same infraction should incur the same result, whether it's a talking-to, a time-out, or a revocation of privileges.

As for caring, that may be the most important thing of all. Do you really care for your children, care about them, and show them that you do? Don't skimp on the hugs, the kisses, the tender touches, and the verbal approbation. If you're proud of them, let them know it. If you approve of them or of something they've done, let them know it. If one of your children takes the initiative and cleans up her room without being asked to, let her know that you noticed and that you appreciate it. And even when they don't do anything special, let them know that you love them and care about them and are proud of them, just because of who they are, and just because you're their mom.

Even if you haven't had much practice at being a mom, that doesn't mean you can't be good at it. Think once again of the executives of companies. No executive was born in that position. Everyone works his or her way up. Most rise through the ranks, from lower positions up to the corner office in the executive suite. Others start small businesses, of which they're the head from day one, and if things go well, the company grows and the owner grows in ability along with the company. But everyone starts somewhere—somewhere lower down the ladder.

How does an executive grow into the position? She assumes the mantle of leadership, believes in her ability to lead well, and tries to learn as much as she can about both the job at hand and the people she has under her.

That's you! The mantle of leadership—motherhood—can rest easily on your shoulders if you have, or develop, self-confidence, and if you learn more about the job at hand and the people in question. In fact, the more you know about your job and your people, the more self-confidence you'll feel. Now, you're ten steps ahead of the game in that you probably know your kids pretty well. In the case of an infant, who is just beginning to exhibit a personality and display some early traits, there's not too much to know yet, but keep your eyes open and learn as you go.

All you need to remember at this juncture, if the child is not your first, is that he is different from his older sibling and should not be expected to develop at exactly the same rate or to exhibit the same tendencies. Just because his older sibling gave up night feedings at a certain age, or was toilet trained at a certain age, is not a reason for you to expect the same thing from this one—or to be cross with him when he doesn't follow suit.

Learning the job is the other part of the equation. Since you're reading this book, you're obviously doing the right thing in trying to read up on how to be a better mother. On-the-job training counts for a lot, too. The old trial-and-error method is time-honored and valuable.

You can learn about your job the same three ways that other executives learn:

- By trial and error, simply doing the job the best way you know how, and learning from the mistakes you'll inevitably commit.
- By reading books and articles that teach you various aspects of your job.
- By talking to other executives (mothers), who can share valuable tips and knowledge with you.

Of course you need to learn how to sift out the advice and ideas you're given, whether from other mothers or from books or articles you read. Not everything will work for your kids, for you as a person, or for your style of parenting. What works for your best friend, and for her kids, may not be best for you. What a parenting expert suggests in a book may not always be best for you either. Always remember that, while there are some hard and fast rules in parenting, there are many more areas in which you have to decide for yourself what the best approach is.

A good executive is flexible and also discerning. She will listen to advice from all sides, be ready to change her management style if she learns a technique that works better than what she's doing now—but she will not listen to everyone about everything and constantly shift her management pattern according to the latest theory she has just read.

This comes right back to self-confidence, the topic of this chapter. If you have confidence in your management style (your parenting style), you will not keep changing it every time someone makes a suggestion or you read another book or article. Adapt only those changes you feel are right for you. Believe in your own abilities and your own instincts. Believe in yourself, and your organization—your children, and your husband too—will believe in you.

Act like a confident leader. Talk like a confident leader. *Lead* like a confident leader. Self-confidence is key for any good executive. Including Mom.

5

YOUR VICE PRESIDENT OF DOMESTIC AFFAIRS

Unless she's the head of a pretty small company, a chief executive is likely to share her responsibilities and her authority with one or more other executives. The corporate hierarchy may include a chair of the board, a president, and a vice president, or the distribution of titles may be different, but the net effect is the same: The chief executive has one or more others at the top with her, sharing in the task of running the company.

In many families, Mom is the one with the primary responsibility for raising the kids, the CEO of the family, but in most families there's a dad too. Even if you're a single mom (divorced, widowed, or never married), though, please read this chapter anyhow. It's certainly possible that, somewhere in the future, you'll be sharing parenting duties with a husband or significant other. And this chapter is about how to do it as seamlessly and frictionlessly as possible.

If you're the family's CEO, at least when it comes to raising the kids, your husband is the vice president of domestic affairs. Depending on your respective personalities, his upbringing, and even to some extent his ethnic background, he may defer to you completely when it comes to parenting decisions, or he may take a very strong leadership role. Most dads fall somewhere in between.

In any business, it helps if the executives are all pulling in the same direction. It helps if the top echelon all have the same, or at least a similar, vision for the company. It helps if they all have similar views on how to achieve their goals. And it helps if they have a similar style of leadership.

In the ideal corporate-styled family scenario—one that bears little relationship to the everyday reality of marriages, I might add—men and women would interview each other extensively before marriage to make sure their parenting styles and views and beliefs are, though probably not totally identical, at least compatible. Before having kids together, they would check out each other's views on parenting, on families, on not just how to raise kids but what their respective goals are for those kids and on all the little minutiae (which, though minute, are very far from trivial!) that make up the fabric of parenting. They might even give each other checklists as well as interviewing each other, to see how compatible are their parenting styles and their goals.

That's some sort of an ideal, but we all know the reality is quite different. Two people in love, who feel they're compatible as a couple, seldom discuss parenting styles before marriage on any but the most surface level, if at all. And even if they were to do so, and to discover that they approach the topic from vastly different viewpoints, it's unlikely that they'd let that impede their marriage. And rightfully so. But it can make for some rocky times down the road, when he and she approach parenting from very different perspectives. Most couples don't discuss the topic more than to agree that they both want kids (or don't), and that two children (or some other number) is probably a good goal to aim for.

In fact, it's rare that both parents have identical approaches. One parent, for example, is almost always more strict than the other. This doesn't have to be a problem, provided they present a united front. But if you mandate a 9:00 p.m. bedtime for Alan, it won't do to have your husband let Alan stay up till 10:00 every time you're at a PTA meeting and he's alone with the kids. If you say, "No candy before dinner," or "Don't eat anything an hour before dinner so you don't ruin your appetite," it's no good for your husband to give Alison a cookie and tell her, with a wink, "This will be our little secret. Don't tell Mom." Now Dad is casting you as the "bad guy" and undermining your authority to boot.

Like most rules, this one does have a few exceptions. One that comes to mind quickly is the father who is adamant that his sixteen-year-old daughter remain a virgin and doesn't want the mother steering the daughter toward any form of birth control. If the mother knows that the girl is, in fact, already sexually active, she had better make sure the girl is protected against pregnancy, and against STDs, too, to the best of the mother's ability to protect her. That may mean taking her to the gynecologist in spite of the father's wishes. But such scenarios are the exception, not the rule.

Let's get back to the subject of vision. Do you and your husband share a similar vision, both for your family as a whole and for each of your kids individually? Just what does each of you want for the family unit and for each child? If you're each steering in a different direction, the ship will surely go off course, and it will be a very difficult journey.

This is true on many levels. Suppose your husband hopes your son will become a professional athlete, but you want him to graduate college and go into a professional career such as doctor, lawyer, or accountant. Of course your son's interests and abilities will play a large part in the final decision. He may, after all, wind up as a musician or a barber! But when you're trying to gently guide him down a career path, it helps if you're both pushing in the same direction. Now suppose you want your daughter to have a fulfilling career and not to marry too early, but your husband thinks that marriage is of paramount importance. Again, you're sending mixed messages to her and probably working against each other's goals as well.

What about the attributes you each think are most important in your kids right now? Suppose you think it's very important for your son to be mannerly and considerate, while your husband wants him to be a rough-and-tumble boy who knows how to defend himself in a fight and doesn't back down from anyone? These are not necessarily mutually exclusive goals, but they certainly are different from each other. Which is the one you're going to tell him is most important? And what if your short-term goals for him *are* in greater conflict with each other? What if you want him to put as much time as possible into his studies, while your husband wants your son to put as much time as possible into sports? When the boy has a half hour at his discretion, you'll be pushing him to open a book and read or learn something, while your husband will be pushing the boy to get outside and shoot hoops or practice pitching a baseball or throwing a football.

What about your vision for the family as a whole? We talked in an earlier chapter about *your* vision for the family, your goals for not just each child but the family as a unit. What are your husband's goals for the family? How do they differ from yours? Are your goals for the family compatible with his? (Differing goals and visions don't have to be mutually exclusive; they can often be compatible and even complementary.)

What are your respective views on how to achieve the goals you've set for each of the kids and for the family as a whole? Do you believe that academics are paramount to the kids attaining their dreams (or your dreams for them)? Or do you think that the best thing for them is to immerse them in as many outside activities as possible, such as music lessons, horseback-riding lessons, after-school sports, crafts classes, and Scouts? Do you believe that learning to socialize successfully with other kids, and learning how to get along with other people, is the single most important thing your kids can learn? Or do you think that simply leading a well-rounded life and having as happy and carefree a childhood as possible is the most important thing to aim for? There is no one right answer; but if you give one answer and your husband gives another, you're going to be pulling in different directions.

Now let's talk about styles of leadership. Is one of you a parent who micro-manages, while the other is a laissez-faire type who believes in letting the kids make many of their own choices? Does one of you believe that the earlier kids learn to make sensible decisions on their own, the better it is, but the other is an authoritarian who insists that parents know best and must make all the decisions? Does one of you believe in strict bedtimes and the other in putting the kids to bed when they look sleepy? Does one of you believe in letting a three-year-old dress herself in anything she wants, provided it's appropriate to the weather, while the other believes she must wear a coordinated, together-looking outfit at all times, chosen by a parent to be certain it looks good? You have differing—and perhaps clashing—styles of leadership.

If the president of a company has a loose style of leadership, while the vice president is rigid, there are going to be some conflicts, both between these two executives themselves and also between them and their employees, who will not be able to please both executives simultaneously. And if two parents have differing styles of leadership, not only will it be difficult for the kids to know how to please them, but the parents themselves are likely to have some friction between them.

It's exceedingly rare that two parents agree totally on rules for the kids, on styles of parenting, on methods of discipline and punishment, and on when punishment is appropriate. Kids have always known that, if they're going to do something out of bounds, they're better off being caught by the more lenient of the two parents, the one who will only lecture but not punish, or the one who will give the milder of two possible punishments. (Conversely, some kids prefer punishment to an "I'm disappointed in you" lecture, which may leave them feeling worse inside.)

If the difference in punishments isn't that great, if Mom takes away a privilege while Dad docks allowance, or Mom says "No TV" while Dad says

"No video games," you don't have a serious problem. But if you think that certain infractions deserve serious punishment while your husband will deal with them only by offering a mild admonition, he is making you look like the "heavy," and this is not the place to be playing "good cop, bad cop." Similarly, if your expectations for the kids' behavior don't agree with each other, you need to come to an agreement on what to tell the kids, even if what you tell them doesn't reflect the true feelings of one or the other of you.

And by "behavior" I mean everything from hitting (Is it *ever* right to hit? What if the other child hits first, and your child delivers a blow in self-defense?) to manners (What's appropriate to expect of a child of this age?) to such courtesies as the handling of visiting relatives (If Aunt Emma comes for the afternoon, is the child expected to sit and make polite conversation throughout the visit, or will you excuse her after ten minutes and let her go outdoors or to her room to do something more enjoyable?).

But even more than agreement on what behavior to expect from a child, how to deal with infractions, what chores are appropriate for a child of a given age, and so on, you really ought to agree on parenting styles.

If, for example, one of you is very directive and the other is more hands-off, or one of you is very authoritarian and believes children should obey their parents with no questions asked and no explanations given, while the other believes kids have a right to understand the reasons behind rules and rulings, you're setting up a situation in which the kids are going to be confused and you and your husband are going to be in conflict. You need to agree on such matters as whether kids have a right to know the reason behind an edict.

By the way, I personally believe it's helpful for kids to understand the reasons behind rules. Beyond the question of whether they're *entitled* to know the reasons, it's *helpful* for them to understand the rationale behind a rule or other edict, whether it's a matter of courtesy or respect or thoughtfulness, a matter of safety, a matter of sensibility, a question of health, or whatever the reason is. I also believe, though, that if the child doesn't understand your reasoning, or doesn't agree with it after having it explained to him, he still needs to do as you say. You're still the parent.

If you believe that kids are entitled to know the reasons behind the rules, and your husband does not, you can try to persuade him of the value in teaching kids the reasons. (They learn more than just "Mom says I have to" or "Dad won't let me." They learn the underlying reasons, which helps them understand manners, or safety, or nutrition, or whatever is at issue here.)

But if he absolutely refuses to give the kids any reason beyond "Because I said so," no matter how persuasively you try to explain the value of offering reasons, there's not much you can do besides offering the kids your own explanations of Dad's rules when asked. This is not undermining Dad's authority, as long as the kids understand that they still must do as Dad mandates. You will try to give them the rationale behind a rule if asked, but whether or not they are given a reason, and whether or not they understand or agree with it, they still must obey Dad's edicts. He's still their parent.

By the same token, you and your husband need to agree that he will back you up even when he doesn't agree with one of your decisions. It might be okay for him to let the kids stay up ten minutes later than their bedtime on occasion, when he's at home with them and you're not. I'm sure you make occasional exceptions to rules also. But he shouldn't make a habit of it so that he comes off looking like the "good guy" and you as the "bad guy." And he certainly shouldn't countermand any major orders of yours. If you've told your son who's of driving age that he's not to use the family car that night, your husband mustn't give your son his clandestine approval, saying, "Just be sure that you have the car back before Mom comes home."

Any disagreements you two have about rules need to be straightened out between yourselves and not disputed in front of the kids. The executives of a well-run business organization adhere to the same tenets, the same rules, the same guiding principles. And the same is true for a family.

Of course you can't anticipate all the points on which you'll differ. Sometimes a situation just comes up and needs to be dealt with on the spot. Say, for example, your four-year-old daughter is invited by a friend to sleep over—her first sleepover date. You're all for it; your husband says, "She's too young." You hadn't anticipated the situation and discussed it in advance. Now you need to discuss it—not in front of your daughter—and agree either to let her sleep over at the friend's or to not allow it. When you agree on a course of action, you need to present a united front. Not "Dad thinks you're too young, but I'm going to let you," or "I'd like to let you, but Dad thinks you're too young." Good executive leadership requires all the executives to present a united front. The "employees" need to feel the management is united in their decisions, even if they realize some differing viewpoints may have been aired before management decided what stance they were going to take.

Let's take one more example of a decision that needs to be discussed in advance: religious upbringing. Many times one parent feels more strongly that the kids should go to religious school and perhaps that the family should attend worship services together. It may be the case that one parent believes that the kids should have a religious upbringing, while the other parent doesn't care about it. It also happens with some frequency that the parents are of different religions, but that's a situation that's more likely to get discussed in advance. Will the kids be brought up Protestant or Catholic, Jewish or Christian? In these cases, the parents have usually discussed the matter beforehand and arrived at some decision. There's actually more chance of dispute when both parents are of the same religious background, but one wants the kids to have some religious education while the other either doesn't care, or actively prefers the kids not to be raised in any religion, or prefers to be able to sleep late Sunday mornings rather than have to get up to take the kids to Sunday school.

How well do you think General Motors, Procter & Gamble, or the small advertising agency in your hometown would run if the CEO ran the company by one set of guiding principles, and one set of rules, and his or her second-in-command had a totally different set of principles and different set of rules? Suppose one believed in flex time—put in your forty hours a week, and it doesn't matter what forty hours you choose—while the other demanded that all work be performed between 9:00 a.m. and 5:00 p.m., Monday through Friday. Whom would the employees listen to? And wouldn't they quickly learn to play one executive against the other?

A family must be run with the same unity at the top. Have your disagreements in the "boardroom," but present a united front to your organization.

6

SHARING
AUTHORITY

Virtually every organization has some sort of "middle management"—people not at the executive level but still in positions of authority. These middle management types hold sway over others but still have to answer to the upper echelon. They don't set policy, but they do get called on to set some rules and to enforce or interpret others, as well as arbitrating disputes among the people they supervise and making sure that those people work properly and conduct themselves according to the company's rules and precepts in the process.

In the corporate world, such people include department heads and other managers. In your "family corporation," you have them, too. Their ranks include babysitters as well as the many others who are responsible to some degree for your kids, and whom your kids have to answer to and follow the edicts of. These include teachers, grandparents, and youth leaders (such as scoutmasters or the leaders of a religion-based youth group), as well as such other people as the parents of your kids' friends, at whose houses they sometimes visit.

All these people will exert some degree of influence over your children and may in some cases set goals or values for them as well as set rules for them.

How do you handle it when another person in authority has a different view of how to manage your kids, or what's best for them, than you do?

Of course, this depends in part on who the person is.

In the business world, you have to give your middle managers, and others with some authority, a certain degree of leeway, a certain amount of autonomy in making decisions. They can't run amok and make decisions that are counter to the company's rules, goals, or precepts. But neither can you stifle their authority or creativity completely. If you micro-manage them and tell them exactly how to run their departments, you might as well not have them there.

So it is, too, in a family. Some of your "middle management personnel" have more authority than others. Obviously it's easier to tell a babysitter what to do or how to deal with your kids than it is to tell a grandparent, whether that grandparent is on your side of the family or your husband's. Teachers and youth leaders fall somewhere in between. They have their own rules to follow, as well as yours, but you can request a meeting with a teacher or youth leader if you think your child is in some way being mishandled or is being taught something counter to your values or precepts. In extreme cases, you can ask to have your child assigned to a different teacher, if you can't reach a meeting of the minds. And you can withdraw him from band, Scouts, after-school groups, or the youth group of your church or synagogue, if you have a serious quarrel with the leader of the group and cannot get him or her to see things your way.

But try not to be so rigid that you get upset if the rules are a little bit different when your child is in someone else's care. First stop and ask yourself how important this rule is and whether it's something that involves your core values or beliefs, or your child's health and well-being. If your three-year-old naps at home from 1:00 to 2:00 but is put in for a nap from noon to 1:00 at day care, he is still getting an hour of sleep. You can't really expect him to nap at a different hour than the rest of the kids in the group, nor is it realistic that the woman running the day care change the time the whole group naps just to accommodate you. Does it really matter that he naps an hour earlier at day care than at home?

If for some reason this is really important to you—if, for instance, he's getting cranky in the evenings—you should first try to find an accommodation, such as putting him to bed a little earlier in the evening. If that doesn't work for you for some reason, you may need to look for a different day-care group to put him in. You can hardly tell the day-care manager to rearrange the schedule of all her charges to accommodate your son.

Let's look at another example. Suppose the day-care manager has a rule that the kids must eat what they're offered for lunch, no substitutions, and this is a facility where the kids don't bring their lunches but rather are served a meal prepared by the day-care center. At home your rule may be that the child must take a taste but then may decline to eat what everyone else is having. Or you may not even have that requirement and may allow him to refuse a meal outright.

Your child needs to learn that he must follow the rules of whoever is in charge of him at the time—even if "middle management's" rules are different from the edicts of the top brass. If you have a serious disagreement with some-one else's rules, you can speak to the person in charge—the day-care manager, in this case—and see if an accommodation can be made. What if you send lunch to school with your child? Will he be allowed to eat that instead? But if you can't work out an accommodation, and "middle management" is being intransigent, you have two choices: either you and your child accept that the rules are different in "that department," or you "fire the manager"—take your child out of that day-care group or after-care group, switch him to another Scout troop, withdraw her from the church's youth group.

When is it worth making an issue over rules that are different from yours? When you believe your child's health or well-being is at risk, or when the authority in question is teaching a set of values that aren't compatible with your own. At one time I had my daughter in an in-home day-care group run by a woman whose boyfriend lived with her. For me, this was no problem at all, nor was it for any of the other parents whose kids were part of this particular day-care group. But if this goes against your core moral values, you may want to put your child in a different group.

Another mother I knew at the time had her kids in an in-home day-care group run by a woman who was deeply religious. This may not sound like a problem, but the day-care leader taught the kids about Jesus, and the mother was Jewish and raising her kids in her religion. She didn't want belief in Jesus inculcated in her child by this day-care manager. Though the level of care and warmth was excellent, and the supervision top-notch, she found herself faced with making the decision to find another group for her child.

What if the problem is with the parent of another child? Your son's friend's mother lets the kids swim in the backyard pool unsupervised, which you don't think they're old enough to do safely. Or what if she allows them to skateboard in the street, which you think is dangerous—this is not a busy thoroughfare but neither is it a quiet cul-de-sac. You can try speaking to this other parent and explaining that you're not comfortable with the level of safety being observed at their house. You can tell her that you don't want your child swimming unsupervised or skateboarding on her street. But what if she's intransigent? Your child needn't totally give up visits with his friend, but you can insist that the friend always visit at your house.

You *are* the boss. You *do* have the right to insist that your child is raised in accordance with your precepts, your values, and your safety rules. But you need to be aware of the difference between trying to make changes in a one-on-one situation and in a group situation. Telling a babysitter what to do and what not to do is fine. Telling grandparents is more problematic but still your right to try. (And if Grandma insists on letting your four-year-old use a sharp knife, you may need to insist that the child visit at Grandma's house only when you are present.) But you cannot insist on a teacher or Scout leader having a different set of rules for your child only.

Your child needs to learn that sometimes the rules change, and he needs to live by the rules in force in the place where he is.

You need to learn when it is worth making a fuss, such as "firing" a day-care manager, Scout leader, or even, in extreme cases, a teacher—by asking the school to change your child to another classroom—and when to let middle management do things their way, as long as the end result is good, the child's safety and health aren't compromised, and your core values aren't being violated.

7

THE TRAITS OF A GOOD CORPORATE EXECUTIVE

Having gotten this far into the book, it should hardly surprise you to read that many of the traits of a good corporate executive are also the traits of a good parent. From leadership skills to organization skills, from being a good listener to being a bold innovator, the same characteristics that are the hallmark of a good corporate executive are also those that help make a mom a better parent.

You need to lead your troops well, understand their needs, know how to motivate them, know when to be stern and when to be sympathetic, always have a goal in mind, keep the good of the organization (family) in sight at all times, and in many other ways take the reins and handle them with all the executive talent you can muster. If you possess the traits of a good corporate executive, or learn to emulate the actions and attitudes of a talented CEO, you'll find that parenting, though it's never an easy endeavor, is a heck of a lot less problematic.

So what are these corporate traits that you want to adopt as your own?

A good corporate executive gets involved in the day-to-day activities of the organization

The best corporate executives don't simply sit in their big corner offices and give orders. They get involved in what goes on in their companies. *This is not the same as micro-managing or doing other people's work for them.* There is a difference. Without taking over someone's work, or telling everyone just how to do their respective jobs, an executive can still observe people at work, ask questions about what's going on and what's being done, inquire about what problems need to be solved, and in this way get a good feel for the day-to-day operations of the company.

Is there a specific problem that a middle manager is dealing with? The corporate executive may have a better idea for how to solve it. (Being a good thinker or problem-solver is probably one of the traits that got her so far up the ladder to begin with.) Is there a situation that the executive observes that she believes needs remedying or changing? Even the physical plant of the company is up for inspection: Should the copying machine be in a more convenient location—or one in which someone with authority can better monitor it for abuse? Should a middle manager's office be more strategically located? Does the reception area present a good first impression of the company to visitors?

A good mom, too, gets involved in the day-to-day activities of her family even when her participation isn't directly called for. Again, this doesn't mean micro-managing or doing her family's tasks for them. But it does mean monitoring performance, for one thing.

You check to make sure that your daughter is washing the dishes, if that's her chore, but do you check periodically to ensure that she's doing a good job? Washing the dishes isn't just about shouldering responsibility for a family task; it's about getting the dishes clean. Is she working properly and effectively, doing a good job, and accomplishing the purpose? Do you merely ask your son if his homework is done, or do you look it over to see what he's accomplished, how good a job he's done, what's he's learning in school, and whether he's writing neatly?

Getting involved with the family's activities also means spending some time with the kids other than at meals and while accomplishing necessities such as bathing really little kids and making sure that tasks are done. When was the last time you played with your kids? (If you're not into video games and you think you'll scream if you have to play Candyland again, how about teaching them a card game or other game from your childhood?)

And how about just *talking*? Not scolding. Not asking, "Did you take your bath yet?" Not reminding, "It's ten minutes till bedtime. Are you ready to get in bed?" Not admonishing, "Your room is a mess and you just cleaned it yesterday." I mean communicating, conversing, interacting with your kids. I mean asking them what's new in their lives, how school was, how their friends are. I mean telling them stories of your childhood, or stories about the extended family—Grandma or Grandpa or Aunt Louise, or the time you and all your cousins went to visit at Gram Edith's house at once. I mean asking them, "Is there anything you want to discuss?" or "Is there any problem you need help with, or any question you want to ask?"

Yes, I know that kids eventually reach an age at which they're non-communicative, answering questions about school, their friends, and their lives in general with monosyllables or mere grunts, and resenting what they claim to perceive as a "cross-examination" if their parents try to make just one or two interested inquiries. Well, you don't need to subject them to the "fifth degree," but you can still show you care about their lives, even if they give minimal responses. (If you stop asking, then no matter how vociferously they've protested the questions, they'll think you no longer care. Really!)

Another way to get involved with the family's day-to-day activities is to ask each child questions about her hobbies and interests, or involve yourself in these if you can. If your daughter is a soccer player, attend some of her games. If you're halfway decent at playing, practice soccer skills with her. If your son plays guitar, ask him to show you how good he's gotten, or if you play guitar yourself, show him some complex fingering or teach him a song he'll recognize but doesn't know how to play. If your daughter collects stamps or coins, ask interested questions about the items in her collection. If your son is an avid reader, ask him about his favorite books or his favorite authors.

And, of course, you can get the kids involved in *your* day-to-day activities as well. How involved and which activities will depend on the ages of your kids and what you have to do. But little ones love "helping Mommy" and even older ones can be drawn into some of your activities happily. Your five-year-old will be happy to hold the dustpan when you sweep; your nine-year-old may be eager to help in the kitchen. Paying bills? It's possible that one of your kids is at an age at which helping by licking the stamps and sealing the envelopes will make him feel important. Balancing the checkbook? Maybe your child is old enough to help you put the cancelled checks in numerical order.

Teenagers are more problematic but not beyond reach. Though they may groan over being asked to help, if you make the project one in which they feel important, not just "used," you may be surprised by the change in attitude. How about asking your teenager for help in planning next week's menus or in planning his younger brother's birthday party?

No, you don't really need your teenager's help in menu planning, and you could do a better job of sweeping if you held the dustpan yourself instead of entrusting it to your five-year-old. And when your nine-year-old peels potatoes for you, she literally peels off part of the potato, not just the skin. But you're working as a team now, fostering a feeling of family, enjoying a time of togetherness, and helping the kids feel useful and needed. And that's more important than a scattering of missed crumbs on the floor, or a chunk of potato that lands in the garbage or down the disposal.

A good corporate executive leads by example

The corporate executive who makes the best impression on her subordinates is the one who doesn't just *tell* them how but *shows* them how. If the company has a goal of reducing money spent on supplies, the executive will take notes on the back of junk mail or old memos. If the company has a goal of keeping the workplace clean, the executive will bend down and pick up that piece of scrap paper on the floor as she passes by.

And you, as a mom in the corporate executive mold, can do the same. I'm sure you insist that your kids get their tasks and their homework and their obligations done on time. But what sort of an example do you set for them? If you're supposed to make a presentation for the PTA, are you prepared in a timely manner, or do the kids see you throwing your facts and your pie charts together hastily at the last minute, in the middle of the dining room table, in a disarray of papers and notes and books? You tell them to get their chores done before a bad situation results, but do they have to sometimes wear dirty clothes to school because you haven't had time to do the laundry?

What sort of example are you setting for your kids?

You counsel them not to take on more things to do than they can handle, to quit the stamp club if it's not going to leave them enough time to do their homework and visit with their friends and do their chores around the house. But do you take on more responsibilities than you can shoulder? If the laundry isn't done, is it because you let yourself get pressured into becoming the chair of the garden club when you knew you didn't really have the time? You tell the kids not to gossip or spread unkind stories about others, but do they hear you on the phone with one of your friends, degrading someone you both know?

What sort of example are you setting for your kids?

After telling your kids to eat healthy snacks and balanced meals, do you let them see you downing a whole quart of rocky road—or eating dinner according to the precepts of the latest fad diet, one that flies in the face of all conventional nutritional knowledge? Do you tell them it's important to eat a good breakfast, then skip breakfast yourself and tell them, "I don't have time"?

What sort of example are you setting for your kids?

You tell your kids that reading is important, but do they ever see you reading anything other than the *TV Guide*? You teach your kids the virtues of charity, but do you practice what you preach by either donating money to charity, or donating time to a worthy cause, giving your old clothes, books, and other resellables to a charity's thrift store, or buying an extra can of sweet potatoes at Thanksgiving and dropping it in the charity food collection carton at the supermarket or bringing it to your church's food pantry?

What sort of example are you setting for your kids?

You tell your kids that it's important to get a good night's sleep. But do you get to bed in time yourself, or do your kids sometimes wake up well past midnight, wanting water or needing to go to the bathroom, only to find you still in front of the TV? (And are you then bleary-eyed and sluggish in the morning, perhaps cross and snappy too, or maybe you oversleep and don't even get them up for school in time?)

What sort of example are you setting for your kids?

You preach patience and calm, but how do you react to the driver who cuts you off when you're driving the kids to school? And speaking of the car, you tell the kids to obey all the rules—both yours and those in school and the laws that apply to them as well, such as if your municipality requires them to wear helmets when they're bicycling—but when they ride with you in the car, do they see you running red lights, responding to stop signs with a "rolling stop," or not ceding the right-of-way where required? What kind of drivers—and what kind of citizens—do you think they'll grow up to be if they follow your example?

What sort of example are you setting for your kids?

A good corporate executive delegates tasks

While a good corporate executive involves herself in the day-to-day running of the business, she doesn't, and can't, and mustn't try to do everything herself. I know of a woman who headed a small business and, rather than explain to her right-hand man (a friend of mine) how to do some of her many tasks, she did them all herself. "It would take too long to explain what I want done" was her rationale. But the result was that she spent most evenings at her desk, working till 11:30 or even till 1:00 a.m. In the end, it took her far longer to complete each task herself. Other misguided executives retain far too much of the workload themselves out of a fear that the job won't be done right if it's entrusted to someone else. "If I do it myself, I know it's getting done right," these people say. But if your business is to grow and prosper, you must let your people expand their assignments and learn how to do more things, freeing you up in turn for more of the executive work.

And if your family is to grow and prosper, your children must learn to take on more responsibility. Maybe dinner can be cooked more quickly, more efficiently, and even more deliciously if you prepare the entire meal yourself. But that isn't teaching your children how to fend for themselves in the kitchen, nor is it teaching them how to be helpful and to shoulder their share of tasks around the house.

Maybe you can do a more effective and thorough job of vacuuming the living room carpet than your child can, but assigning him the job will not only free up some of your time, and free you from a boring task, but will also teach your child a housekeeping skill while teaching him to pitch in and help out with family tasks. You probably will do a better job of washing the dishes than your child can, but if your daughter does the dishes, not only does she learn a needed skill, or get better at performing it, and not only does she understand the importance of pitching in, but you get freed up to sew that merit badge on that Scouts uniform, or to make those phone calls for your civic club, or to feed or bathe the baby, or to "pick up" the living room.

Yes, you're going to have to supervise the kids in their early attempts to help with the laundry, chop onions, dust the shelves, rake the yard, bathe the dog, clean the bathroom mirror, or weed the garden. Yes, it may take you almost as much time as if you were doing the job yourself, and it may be much more frustrating and try your patience no end. And no, the job won't get done perfectly. But the kids need to learn these various skills, you need relief from all these chores, and eventually—believe it or not—the kids *will* learn to do a creditable job at each of these tasks, to the point that you can leave them unsupervised and get some other task accomplished yourself.

Naturally, you need to match the child with an assigned job appropriate for his or her age. You're not going to ask a four-year-old to slice carrots with a sharp knife nor let an eight-year-old paint her own room. But as your kids get older, you can assign them more tasks, and more difficult ones, and free yourself from some of the things that occupy your time now.

It's good for you. It's good for the kids. It's good management.

It's a win-win situation.

A good corporate executive is flexible

When a company's advertising campaign isn't producing the desired results, the head of the company orders the campaign abruptly halted and a new campaign put in place. When a budget turns out to be unrealistic, the CFO or the CEO will often review the budget and see where cuts can be made to allow for greater funding for the items that need it. When a product isn't selling, the CEO may order production of that particular product halted, or have it retooled so it functions better or has a more appealing appearance, or order a new pricing structure to make it more attractive either to the public or to the retailer who sells it and may need more incentive to "push" the product.

If the company has a five-year plan, and midway into the second year it's obvious that things aren't going as they were projected to, a good corporate executive will rethink her plan and change gears. Depending on the nature of the business, the nature of the disappointment, and the other factors that affect the company, the executive may decide to increase or decrease production of one or more products or the availability of a service, hire or lay off employees, raise or lower prices, increase, decrease, or change the level of advertising, close a plant or open one, or simply revise the projections for sales, revenue, and profit (or loss). Other changes may be instituted too. What a good executive *doesn't* do is say, "Well, this is our plan, so we'll stick with it and do the best we can." She's flexible, and she makes changes when circumstances dictate that she needs to.

A good mom needs flexibility even more. To begin with, she mustn't be so hidebound that she does certain things "because I've always done them this way." If you used to serve dinner at 6:00, but this year your son is getting dropped off by the school bus from his new after-care group at 5:45, maybe this year you need to start serving dinner at 6:30 to give your son a chance to "decompress," to get home, put away his jacket and his schoolbooks, use the bathroom and wash his hands, and give you any notes he's brought home from school. Too, you ought to leave a little extra time to allow for those inevitable times when the bus is late dropping him off.

Sure, you've always served dinner at 6:00. But maybe now it's time to change.

Or maybe the situation is that your daughter's every-Thursday band practice doesn't end till 5:30, and then you have to pick her up. In that case, maybe dinner on Thursdays should be at 6:30 or even 7:00, even though you continue to serve at 6:00 the other nights of the week.

Do you have a rule that everybody carries his or her dinner dishes into the kitchen after the meal before doing anything else and helps clear the serving dishes, too? But if you live in an apartment building, and your daughter has started two loads of laundry in the building's laundry room, and it's due out of the washer before dinner's even over, you'd do well to let her go take care of the laundry and *then* come back and clear her dishes. You don't want the laundry disappearing or the last dryer being taken while she's adhering strictly to your rules. Do you have a rule that the kids are allowed only one hour of TV-watching per weeknight? Is there an educational (or otherwise worthwhile) special program on tonight that lasts two hours? If it won't interfere with their bedtimes, or their getting their homework finished, you can bend the rules this once.

If your son's bedtime is 8:30, but it's the first warm night of spring and he wants to spend some time outdoors, and it's a Friday, so there's no school tomorrow, consider letting him stay up a little late this once. He can sleep late in the morning and still get his full complement of sleep.

Sometimes flexibility involves not just your own children but their friends or other visitors. When my daughter was two, I was newly divorced and involved with a new man in my life. My daughter and I were invited for dinner to the home of this man's sister and her family (a husband and two very young boys). My daughter, who had eaten all she cared to of the main course, grew restless sitting at the table as we adults talked. She asked me if she could leave the table. I turned to my host and hostess and asked their permission, which they gave, so I helped my daughter out of her chair, and she went off to play with one of the boys' toys. The main course was eventually followed by dessert, and when it was served, naturally my daughter wanted some. She climbed back onto her chair and was dismayed to hear our host and hostess proclaim that she wouldn't be allowed any dessert. The rule in their household (which had not been told to any of us!) was that anyone who left the table was not entitled to eat dessert.

Naturally she wailed and carried on, but our host and hostess, saying they didn't want to set a bad precedent for their boys, refused to bend the rule. I thought it was unfair, given that the rule had not been told to us before my daughter got out of her chair. Needless to say, the rest of the evening was an unhappy one. The real error was in not telling my daughter of this rule before excusing her from the table. But I think the lack of flexibility was an error, too.

Do you require your kids to eat their vegetables? What do you do when a friend of theirs visits who doesn't like spinach, refuses to eat it, and insists that at home he doesn't have to? A little flexibility is in order. Sometimes compromise is the answer. Or suppose that your son has a friend sleep over, and your son's bedtime is 8:00, while the friend is allowed to stay up till 9:00. As long as it's not a school night, you might allow a compromise of 8:30.

Though a good corporate executive always has a plan, she doesn't follow it slavishly. If it isn't working, or if circumstances change and dictate that she alter her thinking, she's not so hidebound that she won't or can't change course. Whether the need for change is brought about by an overall downturn in the nation's economy, a competitor's bringing out a similar product, an employee's suggesting a new product worth producing, a bad report on the test of a new service with a focus group, a hike in the cost of raw materials, or other causes, the executive will answer the challenge by changing her plans—radically if need be.

Moms, too, need to be flexible enough to change plans, both large and small, short-term and long-term, when things aren't going as expected. If Kayla's softball game ran late, and you haven't time to get the stuffed peppers prepared and cooked and on the table by 6:00, don't get upset at the delay; just go to Plan B. "Plan B" might involve eating dinner at 7:00, or it might mean your preparing some tuna salad, a mixed green salad, and some nuked baked potatoes for dinner instead of the stuffed peppers.

All too many moms let themselves get flummoxed by such events. The trick is to remember what good corporate executives do: don't be perturbed, just go to Plan B. You may not have a Plan B at the ready, but if you stay calm and think for a minute, you can usually come up with one, whether it's delayed dinner, tuna salad, or takeout. (Haven't the kids been clamoring for pizza for weeks now anyhow?)

Did the babysitter disappoint you? Again, deviate from your plan instead of being upset. If you can reschedule your plans to go out and pick another night when she expects to be available, do so. If the plan was to go to a dinner party at some friends', which can't be rescheduled, can you get another sitter? Call Grandma to the rescue? Find friends the kids can spend the night with?

Did your son break his arm skateboarding, and did the resultant trip to the E.R. totally wreck your budget for the week? Revise your plan for the week's dinners and prepare the lowest-cost menus you can dream up. Even if you can't save an amount equal to what the medical bills cost, you'll save back a chunk of it. Put aside your menu plan and accompanying grocery list to use some other week down the road. Planning it wasn't a wasted effort. You'll use it a month from now. For now, you're looking at creative ways to cook pasta differently yet inexpensively, but instead of feeling frazzled by the sudden budget problem, feel good about your creativity as you rise to the occasion with a low-budget, tasty menu.

Did Jennifer get sick the day you were to leave for vacation? Did Austin turn stubborn about potty-training and refuse to learn to use the toilet in time for his entry into the day care that demands all its kids be potty-trained? Is Cassie insisting she doesn't want the type of birthday party you've planned for her because it's "lame and babyish," even though it's exactly what she said she wanted when you discussed it four months ago?

These situations all create major disruptions in your plans, and you'll need to change your plans in the face of these events. If you don't have a Plan B in mind, start thinking of one when the problem occurs, instead of just wringing your hands and saying, "Now what am I going to do?" Better to ask yourself that very question literally: *Now what are you going to do?* And then answer it.

Did the gold-star system that worked so well with Melanie for rewarding good manners fail miserably with Amanda? Did the system of taking away privileges that worked so well in disciplining Rob fail you utterly with Andy? Change your plan. Don't stick with something that isn't working.

A good executive is always willing and able to go with a different plan when necessary.

A good corporate executive has a plan

Actually a good corporate executive has any number of plans, short-range and long-range both. She has a plan for what she's going to do today. She has a plan for how she's going to deal with the discontent arising among certain of the personnel. She has a visionary, far-reaching plan for the company's future. She has a plan for the next year that encompasses growth, production, income, expenses, personnel enhancement, incentives, and much more. She has a strategy for making her company more competitive with its rivals. She has alternatives in mind for handling the potential shortages in raw parts coming from suppliers overseas. She has plans galore.

Moms need to have a plan, or a bunch of plans, as well. You need plans for saving money for the kids' college (or technical school) and plans for saving money for "rainy day" emergencies, for buying a bigger house, for the inevitable next car, for family vacations, and for miscellaneous purposes. And, speaking of money, you need a budget (that's a type of plan, too) for the more immediate period of time: this week, or this month, or both. Getting by by the seat of your pants from week to week seldom cuts it.

You need other types of plans too. If you have small kids, you need a plan for what to do if you become separated from one of them in public. Do they know what to do if they become lost on the street or at an amusement park or in a store? Did you plan ahead and instruct them on what to do in that circumstance? And speaking of emergencies, does your family practice disaster drills such as fire drills? If you live in a part of the country where tornadoes or earthquakes are a hazard, add drills for those emergencies to the list of things you need to practice for with your kids. Have a plan for the family so each member knows what to do if he or she smells smoke or sees flames, or in case of a tornado or earthquake.

There are other types of contingencies you also need to rehearse for with the kids: These include what to do if they're home alone and the doorbell rings, or someone calls on the phone, and what to do if a stranger offers them a ride (or uses one of the more common luring ploys on them while they're outdoors without you, such as, "Will you help me find my lost puppy?" or "Your mom sent me to pick you up"). You need to have a plan for your kids for each of these circumstances and to rehearse it with them from time to time.

Even teenagers need a variety of "emergency rehearsals." What are they expected to do if they are out with a friend old enough to have a license who is responsible for driving them and who gets hold of a can of beer or two and starts drinking? What should they do if a friend offers them beer, hard liquor, or drugs? What should a girl do if out on a date with a guy who either gets sexually demanding, gets nasty and insulting, or in some other way makes her uncomfortable? You need to formulate a plan with your kids for each of these contingencies and any others that seem possible. Make sure they know what you want them to do if they find themselves in one of these predicaments.

For that matter, younger kids can find themselves in tight spots too. What if your eleven-year-old is at his friend's house, and the plan was for the friend's mom to bring him back home at 6:00, but he realizes she's had several drinks and is walking and talking "funny"? What if your fourteen-year-old is with her friend and the friend's dad, and the dad's driving is terrible? He's weaving all over the road, taking terrible chances in cutting in and out of lanes—not drunk, just a dangerous driver?

Or what if the dad touches her inappropriately? (For that matter, you need to teach your younger kids, too, about "good touch, bad touch," and what to do if someone touches them in a way or in a place that makes them uncomfortable.)

You need to rehearse with them. You need to have a plan.

On a more mundane level, you need a day-to-day plan—a Things to Do list. You may want one list for all the things you need to accomplish (not just today but altogether) and another for today's set of tasks, chores, errands, and meetings. Planning ahead will help you avoid forgetting to pick up the dry cleaning, forgetting that Thomas has no clean PJs and you need to do laundry, forgetting that you need to start dinner early because Beth has choir practice at 6:30, or forgetting that you should pick up that gallon of milk on the way home from work or on the way home from picking up the kids at school.

If you're a stay-at-home mom, you need a plan for how you're going to spend the afternoon with your small child, and if that plan is dependent on the weather or on another person, you need a Plan B in case of rain, in case of a no-show by the boy with whom your three-year-old had a playdate, or in case of any other factor throwing a monkey wrench into the works.

If you're the mother of a small child, you need a plan for how you're going to keep him amused while you cook dinner.

You certainly need plans for the weekend, every week. This may involve planning ahead to get a babysitter so you can go out Saturday night, or planning ahead to see if your son and daughter can stay with friends overnight while you're out. (Or while you and your husband enjoy a quiet or romantic evening home alone.) Certainly you know what it's like to try to find a babysitter on short notice! When you have no plans and no intention of going anywhere, and you get a last-minute invitation, scrambling to find a sitter or make other suitable arrangements may be necessary; but if you know that you have theater tickets, a party, a concert, a barbecue, or a casual but all-adults get-together with friends scheduled for an upcoming evening, it pays to arrange for a sitter (or other coverage for your kids) as far in advance as is feasible.

And arranging for a sitter isn't all you need to do in planning your weekend. To avoid dealing with bored kids, you need to have a plan to keep them occupied. I don't mean that you have to structure their days with activities scheduled by the quarter hour! But do have at least some idea of what they're going to do this weekend. By the time they're teenagers, they can make their own plans, unless there's something you need to involve them in: a visit to Aunt Linda's house, a shopping expedition to buy new jeans for them, or a family excursion they won't want to miss out on, such as a visit to an amusement park. You need to plan by telling them well in advance that on Sunday afternoon Uncle Tim and the boys are coming over, and you expect your kids to be there.

And if they're younger than teenagers? Then, as I said, you need to have some sort of plans, not for their every waking minute but enough to ensure that they aren't bored out of their skulls—and that they don't make your day miserable as a result. "Plans" does not necessarily imply going somewhere or even doing "fun" things. Plans might include a trip to the supermarket to buy a week's worth of groceries, with the kids in tow, perhaps with a promise that each can buy one reasonably priced impulse item if they behave themselves. Plans might include a Saturday afternoon cleanup with everyone pitching in.

But plans can be fun, too. Your plans for the weekend for your family might include lunch in a "family restaurant," or a trip to the movies or the local arcade or the miniature golf course, or even a trip to the nearby airport to see the planes take off and land. Another plan for fun that's inexpensive is a comic-book-buying expedition. The kids will enjoy buying the comics as well as taking them home to read. (And reading is certainly a good thing; if your kids are reluctant readers, remember that reading a comic book is better than not reading anything at all.)

Or your plans for your kids might need to be of the type that keeps them busy while you get something done on your own. Perhaps you have a report for work that you must get done this weekend, or perhaps it's time for spring cleaning this weekend, or perhaps you simply have myriad tasks and chores, from balancing the bank statement to paying bills to baking for the church bake sale to getting after that sewing pile that's slowly growing into a small mountain. You know you'll manage to spend some time with your kids, but for a large chunk of time, you're going to be occupied doing other things, and you need to keep them involved and out of your hair. So you plan ahead by inviting friends over to play with them, or by renting a couple of suitable movies, or by setting up the bridge table, draping a sheet over it, and thus providing them with a house or fort to play in.

You need to plan ahead for every summer, too. The kids are going to be out of school; they need something more to do than just sit around the house, watching TV all day. Depending on their ages, your financial circumstances, whether you work, where you live, and whether your husband gets vacation time off during the summer, your summer plans for the kids may include sending them off to sleepaway camp, sending them to your town recreation department's day camp or your local school's summer program, sending them to a for-profit day camp, sending them to Scout camp, sending them or taking them to visit Grandma and Grandpa, taking a family vacation with them to a kid-friendly destination, or simply spending a summer at home with a good mix of structured time and free time, with plenty of trips to the shore or the lake, the zoo and the library, the child-oriented events at your local bookstore, and whatever other opportunities your locale offers, as well as plenty of time for the kids to just play in the backyard, go out on their bikes, and spend time with friends who are also home for the summer. In fact, your plans for the summer may include a mix of these things: four weeks at sleepaway camp, two weeks on a family vacation, one week visiting Grandma and Grandpa, and the rest of the time spent doing things at home and around your area. But however you structure their summer, you need to have a plan.

From planning menus to planning outings to planning ahead for the future, you need a "road map" of where you're going, what you need to do, and what your family is going to be doing. Although you need to not be rigid—and we'll get to that in just a minute—it helps to have a plan of action, short- and long-range plans, emergency plans, and other types of plans so you're not caught flatfooted and unprepared.

A good corporate executive isn't afraid to deviate from her plan

When a company's advertising campaign isn't working, when a budget-imposed hiring freeze leaves a company short-staffed and unable to fill open positions, when a new customer turns in a huge order to a manufacturing concern and the factory can't produce the product fast enough, when a public relations firm takes on a new client and prepares an extensive campaign, only to have an old scandal get unearthed and besmirch the client's name, making hash of the campaign, plans have to be changed. A good corporate executive has a plan, but she also isn't afraid to change it.

It's entirely too easy for many people to stick to a plan once they have one, whether or not that plan is a good one. Many people find it difficult to change their thinking. Whether a plan is comfortable because it's always worked before or whether it's comfortable simply because it's easier to stick to an already-devised plan than to come up with a new one, the fact is that too many people are way too reluctant to change gears. But a good corporate executive knows that if a plan isn't working well, or isn't working well enough for her purposes, it's time to rethink. And an effective mom knows she needs to do the same.

What sort of plans need changing? Any type of plan—from day-to-day routines to a Things to Do list to a budget—can require a change of thinking, a change of action, a change of plan. Suppose dinner has always been served at 6:00, followed by Mom's doing the dishes while Dad bathes the three-year-old; then Mom puts the little one to bed and checks over the seven-year-old's homework before letting him watch an hour of television pre-bed.

Many factors might make this routine, once a good one, no longer optimal.

- Dad might have a change of job or other change in work routine that now has him arriving home at 6:00, and he doesn't like to eat the minute he walks in the door. He wants time to "decompress" first.
- Or Mom might be the one who changes jobs or job schedules and can no longer comfortably have dinner on the table at 6:00.
- The three-year-old might change day-care centers and now needs to be picked up by Mom at 5:30, which precludes having dinner on the table at 6:00.
- Or, continuing in that vein, the three-year-old's change of day-care centers might have her now needing to be dropped off at an earlier hour in the morning, which means getting her to bed earlier at night, which in turn requires feeding her dinner earlier. Either the whole family will have to eat earlier, or if Dad isn't home early enough for that, that child may have to eat earlier than the rest of you, or the two kids might eat earlier while the parents eat separately later. (Weekend dinners would then be something of an Occasion, with the whole family eating together.)
- The seven-year-old might find, in the fall, when he starts a new grade in school, that his new teacher gives more homework. No longer is he finished with homework and ready to have it checked over after dinner; he's still working on it.
- This same older child might become old enough to be tasked with doing the dishes, relieving Mom of the necessity of washing anything but sharp knives and pans with stubborn baked-on foods.
- New work hours for Dad, or a divorce, or other circumstances might result in his not coming home for dinner with the family nor being

there to help bathe the younger child. Now Mom needs to take on that task, and perhaps this means leaving the dishes piled up in the sink until later.

Without having to tax my imagination very greatly, I could easily think of other scenarios that could cause a need for a change of routine as well, but you get the idea: what has worked fine in the past as a routine for you may no longer work well and may require your rethinking your routine.

What other types of plans might need changing? Well, how about your approach to dealing with disciplinary or behavioral problems? If your three-year-old is suddenly throwing temper tantrums, or hitting, or biting, if your seven-year-old persists in chewing with his mouth open or belching loudly with his mouth uncovered, if your nine-year-old lies or is spiteful, you probably have a plan for dealing with the problem.

Whether your approach is giving reasoned explanations of why this behavior is unacceptable, or imposing time-outs, or giving the child some form of punishment such as loss of privileges (or perhaps your approach is a combination of these), you have a methodology you follow—a plan. But what if the plan doesn't work? What if the temper tantrums, hitting, biting, open-mouthed chewing, loud belching, lying, or spitefulness continues? A quote most often attributed to Einstein reads, "Only a fool keeps doing the same thing and expects different results." You're no fool, so if the plan by which you've been handling your child's behavioral or disciplinary problems doesn't work, after a reasonable while of course you're going to try a different plan and see if you get better results.

Sometimes the plan that needs changing is as simple as a plan for how you're going to spend your Saturday. A child with the sniffles or an upset tummy, a bad headache that suddenly hits you, inclement or unseasonably cold weather, a child who begs to be allowed to visit a friend despite your having planned a family outing, Dad's having to unexpectedly work on a Saturday when you'd planned a family outing, or a sick dog who needs to be taken to the vet (or watched closely at home) are just some of the contingencies that can foul up your well-thought-out plan.

Or, if your three-year-old and your four-year-old both wet their beds Saturday night, you may find you need to give the kids baths first thing Sunday morning and then do laundry right after breakfast, when you'd planned to go to the supermarket. Now your supermarket trip is delayed, which causes you to serve lunch late. No time to whip together the chicken salad and potato salad you were planning on making—not if you want to have lunch at a semi-reasonable hour. So lunch is a bit later than you (and the kids) would have liked, and the menu is different, too. (If you think about it while you're in the supermarket, you can buy some hot dogs or cold cuts or something else to serve for lunch, which means your shopping list is also getting altered by the unexpected contingency. Another plan that you're changing!)

If lunch runs late enough, it may impact your afternoon plans: no time to do all four things you'd intended to do. You need to pare down your list, whether it was a list of fun places to take the kids, a list of chores to do around the house, or some of each. And if you serve lunch significantly late, your family and you may not be hungry for dinner at the usual hour. This means either serving later than you usually do or else serving a smaller meal—either cooking fewer dishes or preparing smaller portions. See how one event—two kids wetting their beds—has a cascading effect on your whole day? Politicians call this "the domino effect." Most moms call it "dealing with real life." The bottom line is that when stuff happens, plans have to be changed.

Economic plans, too, may go haywire on you. You may have a plan to put so much money every week in the college tuition fund, so much money in the family vacation fund, and so much money in the checking account for general purposes. Then Fluffy, your cat, gets hit by a car, or Jonny, your nine-year-old, gets a broken arm that isn't fully covered by insurance, or your husband gets laid off, or you do, or your parents suddenly need financial help from you, or . . . well, you get the idea. Suddenly your financial plans are all askew.

Your plans for your children's future, too, may come a cropper. You think your child is going to be a scientist, but suddenly she grows enamored of the theater and declares her new ambition is to become a playwright or actress. Your son the computer genius suddenly develops an interest in photography, and your plans for him to become a programmer are gone with the wind, in the wake of his interest in becoming a paparazzo or a photojournalist.

There are many other examples of plans that may need to be changed, but you get the idea by now. No matter how good a plan you devise, it may not work out in the face of day-to-day happenings, changed circumstances, or other factors beyond your control, often factors that can cause the best-crafted plan to fail to bring the desired results. What do you do in such a case? You have to be flexible and go with Plan B (or Plan C or D) or devise an alternate plan if you don't have one at the ready. You can't stubbornly stick to the old plan or insist on trying to make it work despite the new circumstances or the fact that the plan obviously isn't working.

A good corporate executive expects to be recognized and followed as the leader— and takes appropriate steps when her people get out of line

No matter how democratically an office is run (and some are run far more democratically than others), there is at least one boss (and, in a large concern, several levels of bosses). In a family, too, whether it's closer to the authoritarian end of the continuum or closer to the democratic end, someone has to be recognized as the Boss. In the typical two-parent family, there are, of course, two bosses, but Mom is usually more actively involved in "managing" the kids.

In a corporation, employees who don't respect the boss's authority are dealt with in ways ranging from being talked to to being demoted to being fired. While you can't fire a child and banish him from the family, you *can* and *should* take other corporate-style steps with a child who refuses to acknowledge your authority. What those steps are will depend on whether we're talking about a three-year-old, a ten-year-old, or a fifteen-year-old, whether this is a "first offense" or repeated, and whether it's a serious infraction or a minor one.

It may be that all that's needed is a heart-to-heart talk. It may be that the flaw is in *you*—that you haven't been projecting self-confidence, or you have been making rules, then letting the kids get away with flouting them, leading them to see you as an ineffective, weak leader who needn't be obeyed. Or it may be that the child is stubborn, defiant, and unruly and needs to be reminded of who's boss—through the loss of privileges, through docking of allowance, through punishment, through a verbal expression of extreme displeasure on your part, or through some combination of these.

A good corporate executive knows how to listen and observe

Though a good corporate executive remains in charge at all times, that doesn't mean that she's being directorial at all times. She knows that sometimes she needs to be quiet and listen, watch, and learn what's going on around her. To keep things running well, she needs to be aware of what her people are doing. And sometimes that means being unobtrusively observant.

A mother, too, needs to observe her people in action. I am not referring here to simply making sure that the baby isn't sticking keys in the electrical outlet. I am talking about learning more about your kids by observing the way they relate to each other and to the world around them.

You may think you know your kids and their personalities, but since kids change as they grow and evolve, what you think you know about Sara, who is four, may really be what was true of her when she was three and a half, and it may not be valid anymore.

You may know that your two sons fight, and you may know that Evan is usually the instigator, but are you aware of all the subtle little things that Michael does to "push Evan's buttons" until Evan can't take any more and erupts?

Have you ever stopped to consider that Lisa relates to new things by touching them and Ryan by observing them?

If you know that Mindy is a risk-taker who welcomes new experiences but Alan is cautious, conservative, and hesitant to try new things, do you also know what this means about the best way to introduce new foods to them?

Have you ever listened to the kids playing, or just talking, when they don't realize you're within earshot around the corner? What can you learn about their feelings, their fears, their thoughts, and about the way they interact with each other when they don't realize they're being observed?

Have you ever stopped to think that even though Colin is a bit of a bully toward his younger brother and orders him around, he might be a natural leader, and the better approach toward handling Colin might be to teach him tact rather than to try to stop him from bossing his brother around altogether?

Being a good corporate leader of your family involves listening and watching and drawing your own conclusions about what you've observed, not just being directive.

The good corporate leader listens to suggestions, too.

Again, this is often a matter of how much self-confidence an executive has. The executive who believes in herself and has confidence in her leadership ability is not afraid to listen to suggestions and sometimes amend procedures accordingly. Similarly, the mom who is secure in her authority is not afraid to let the kids speak up and make suggestions.

The suggestion may be for a better way to divide the chores fairly. The suggestion may be for an earlier or later dinnertime. The suggestion may be for an activity for the weekend that's fun: "Let's go see that new movie this weekend," or "Can we go to the arcade on Saturday?" The suggestion may be for a summer vacation destination (probably a request to go to Disney World!). It may be, "Let's buy another computer, so I don't have to fight to get my homework done when Bruce is playing games." Or the suggestion may be, "Let's buy a bigger house so I can have my own room" or "Let's move to Topeka so we can live near Nana and Pop-pop."

Executives sometimes install suggestion boxes, in which employees can leave suggestions anonymously. That's a much less useful procedure in a family, where everyone's handwriting is recognizable to you, but the idea of encouraging suggestions is a good one, albeit by a different method. There is a downside to encouraging suggestions, though: When suggestion after suggestion is turned down, the kids may wonder whether it's worth trying.

If yours is a family that has weekly (or monthly) Family Council meetings, these are a good venue for bringing up suggestions (and also grievances). Just as at a staff meeting in an office, questions, complaints, suggestions, and other situations can be brought up, discussed, and sometimes acted on. And in the relative calm of a council meeting, you're more likely to listen fairly to suggestions. When a child hits you with a suggestion while you're trying to get dinner together, answer a constantly ringing phone, chase down a toddler who's suddenly suspiciously quiet, and call out answers or hints to your child who keeps asking for homework help, you're not likely to be very receptive to the suggestion at hand (or to much of anything else). In a more conducive venue, an orderly meeting, your child and his idea get a much fairer shot at approval.

And who knows? Just as the employees sometimes come up with suggestions that are worthwhile, your kids can do so also. So, regardless of where the idea is presented to you—at a Family Council meeting, in the family van on the way to the soccer game, or in the living room in the middle of a raging argument—open your ears, open your mind, and listen. Unless the idea is totally out of the question, consider it before you say no. (And if you must say no, it's good if you can give some explanation for the turndown. This needn't lead to an argument back and forth. If the child persists in debating you, answer, "I said no, and I explained why. Now drop it.")

But kids will be much more willing to follow with much less resentment if they feel their voices will be heard and their ideas and thoughts considered. Again, though, that doesn't mean you have to accept every suggestion offered.

A good corporate executive
thinks outside the box

Creativity isn't only for the rank and file, whom we were just talking about. Creativity is much prized in executives. And one outgrowth of creativity is thinking outside the box. A good corporate executive, faced with a challenge, a question, a situation, or a dilemma, will think not only of solutions that are conventional or that have worked before but also of new and different solutions. What *might* work?

Whether the challenge is in new product development, in dealing with an unpleasant and untrue story about the company that's making the rounds (such as that old canard about Procter & Gamble being allied with the devil), in employee relations, or in coping with competitors, a top-drawer executive lets her thinking range far afield. In seeking a strategy to use in dealing with the situation at hand, she considers not only what has worked before, for her or for others, but new, different, even offbeat approaches.

Executive Mom should do the same. For example, let's say Scott persists in chewing with his mouth open. Countless times, Mom has reminded him not to do that and has explained how unpleasant it is to watch. When innumerable reminders fail to effect a change in her son, Mom decides to try punishments and institutes a system of withholding privileges. Yet even that fails to bring about the desired change; Scott still chews with his mouth open.

Okay, it's time to think outside the box. The standard means of solving the problem aren't working. How about placing a stand-up mirror on the table right in front of Scott and letting him see just how gross he looks? If that just encourages him, how about rigging a makeshift curtain out of a pillowcase and two wire coat hangers and placing this curtain in front of Scott on the table, telling him it will be removed once he learns to eat in a manner that won't gross out the others at the table? And if that fails to have the desired effect? Maybe he's taking too-large mouthfuls, which is causing the problem, and he needs, rather than to be chastised or punished, to have his eating habits corrected. Maybe he's taking too-large bites because he's rushing through dinner for some reason. (To be excused from the table so he can play video games?) Telling him he has to stay till everyone's finished eating would solve that problem. Maybe a reward for those kids in the family who exhibit good table manners is the ticket to improving his chewing habits.

And speaking of eating, my own mother thought just a bit outside the box when it came to getting me to eat my veggies. When I was in my teens, asparagus was the only green vegetable I was willing to eat, and how many nights a week does a mother want to serve and eat asparagus?! Yet she wanted me to have a green vegetable every night. No matter what she cooked, I turned up my nose at it, till she remembered that I loved salad. Now, salad isn't your conventional cooked green veggie, but it is a veggie (or actually a mixture of several), it is predominantly green, and it is healthy. And my mother had no problem with eating salad night after night herself.

So every night my mother made salad, and every night I ate salad—with gusto—and got my daily requirement of green vegetables. If my mother had a yen for peas or string beans or limas for herself, she made some of those, too (but not enough for me—why waste food?), so she didn't have to be bored eating only lettuce. It wasn't conventional to serve both a veggie and a salad at family dinner tables, any more than it was conventional to serve salad night after night after night after night. But it solved the problem, and it did so happily. After years of fruitlessly trying to get me to eat vegetables, my mother found the answer once she thought outside the box. (And still later, she discovered that while I hated plain spinach, I would eat creamed spinach very happily. Another veggie she could add to the menu!)

What's *your* dilemma? If the standard remedies, the standard answers aren't working for you, it's time to think outside the box. Be creative. Be original. Be different. And be productive.

A good corporate executive has good character

A good corporate executive, who expects good character from her people, knows she must demonstrate the same quality in herself. Her people look to her as a role model, look up to her for leadership, and will follow her example. If she backstabs, deals dishonestly, is intolerant, plays favorites, or in any other way displays bad character, her workers will think the same type of behavior is acceptable in them. What's more, she won't inspire them to give her their best work. Lacking the needed respect for her, they won't give one hundred percent to their work.

And a mother who is trying to raise her children to be good people and good citizens must also display good character. How can you teach a child to always be truthful if you also say to her, "Answer the door, and if it's Emily Turnbull, tell her I'm lying down with a headache"? (This is assuming you're not lying down, and your head feels perfectly fine.) How can you teach a child not to shoplift when you bring her shopping with you and, in front of her, you ask the supermarket cashier to credit you for a coupon for a product you haven't actually bought? That's also a form of stealing, a point that, depending on the child's age, may not be lost on her. How do you teach acceptance of people of all kinds if you have and display prejudices of your own? How do you encourage any aspect of having a good character if your own character needs working on?

Even such a relatively small flaw (because it's not an honesty issue or fairness issue) as giving in easily to temptation, or lacking willpower, is discernible to your kids. If you complain that you weigh too much, but you keep eating chocolates, or you keep dipping into the ice cream in the freezer, or cutting slice after slice of cake, you're sending your kids a message. Having good self-control and willpower are marks of good character too. And when you get on your kids' cases for eating too much candy, or for lacking self-control in some other facet of their lives, remember the example you've been offering them.

Any child's first role model is his or her mother. A mother must live up to the challenge and rise above herself. She has to be not only the kind of person whose character inspires faith in her leadership but the kind of person whose character her children can emulate.

As small children, your kids will follow your example. The danger in not having a good character is in the kids growing up similarly lacking. The hazard increases as they get older; now you need to be concerned that, if better role models inspire them to rise above the bad character traits they've copied from you, they'll look down on you for your flaws. You don't want your children thinking ill of you because you lack good character. So, if you need to, clean up your act!

A good corporate executive seeks opportunities for corporate growth

Corporate growth can take many forms. It can mean adding new people to the organization, or producing more products, or selling them in new markets, or simply learning new things about your organization, your people, your markets, or your marketing techniques.

Family growth can take many forms as well. Obviously having more children is one form of "growing a family," but it is hardly the only way in which a family can grow. A family grows by having new experiences and learning new things. If you live in a nice part of town and take the kids on an expedition to the inner city to show them that not everyone lives as they do, you're expanding their knowledge and their understanding of the world around them. That's a form of growth. If you send them to their cousin's farm in Iowa because, as city kids, they think milk comes from the supermarket and know nothing about cows and farming, that's growth. If you take one part of your backyard and devote it to a vegetable garden, so the kids can labor to produce some of what goes on the table, that's a new experience, a learning experience, and is family growth. If the kids go to your office, or your husband's place of business, whether it's an office, an auto repair garage, or otherwise, and learn just what an executive, an engineer, an accountant, an auto mechanic, an architect, or a commercial fisherman does, or just what it's like to be in a business atmosphere, that's a growth experience.

A family grows by having new experiences and learning new things. If your family isn't religious, but you take the kids to church one day so they can see what a worship service is like, that's a growth experience. If you're Methodists and you take them to a Baptist service so they can see how others worship, that's a growth experience. (If you take them to a Roman Catholic church, a Jewish synagogue, or a Muslim mosque, that's even more of a growth experience.)

Other growth experiences include teaching something more about being "green" (and I don't mean it in the sense that Kermit the Frog sings), something more than just tossing appropriate containers in the recycle bin, that's a growth experience. If they're old enough for you to bring them to help out in the serving line at a soup kitchen, that's a growth experience. So are expeditions to science or natural history museums, or other educational venues.

Any experience or discussion that leads to better compassion or empathy, better understanding of others who are different in any way, or a desire to be helpful to this world and the people in it is growth. So is anything that teaches more about the family, such as your drawing a family tree and helping the kids understand who their relatives are and how they are related to each other. Other such examples include paging through a family photo album and pointing out the faces in it and telling the kids stories about these people, and telling the kids bedtime stories about your childhood, or the family's history, some nights, in lieu of telling them fairy tales or reading them stories from *Robin Hood* or other favorite books.

A good corporate executive
knows how to motivate

We touched on the subject of motivation in the last item. But let's take the subject a little further. A good corporate executive knows that employees can't be rewarded for every accomplishment with a raise, a bonus, or a promotion. She has to depend on other forms of encouragement for day-to-day motivation. Other than simply through praise and recognition, how will she accomplish this?

There are various other perks that are commonly used in the corporate world, from plaques to "Employee of the Month" and "Employee of the Year" awards to temporary ownership of coveted parking spaces (close to the entrance, or under an overhang that protects in inclement weather, or marked "Reserved for the Employee of the Month," or an otherwise especially desirable parking space).

Moms, too, can find ways to acknowledge exemplary behavior overall, or a particular exemplary event, on her kids' part. Of course, the child who always does all his chores, does them well, and does them without being asked might be deserving of a raise in allowance to recognize that fact. But there are other ways to recognize kids' accomplishments, achievements, and overall good behavior.

For generations, parents have been giving their kids gold stars for good behavior, and this method still works with young kids today. You can create a construction-paper "certificate" honoring Jeffrey for keeping his room clean for an entire week. Tape the certificate to the door of his room or hang it on the fridge. If yours is a family that has weekly Family Council meetings, verbal recognition and approbation at the meeting can make his chest swell with pride (and inspire him so that he's determined to continue keeping his room clean). You can also reward a child by excusing him from a chore: "Thank you for making dinner for your brother while I was lying down not feeling well. It was very thoughtful of you. And it was good of you to keep him occupied and let me sleep. Now take the evening off from doing the dishes. I'm feeling better, and I'll do them for you."

Just as an honored employee gets a special space to park in, an honored child can have a special seat at the table, or a special chair to sit in, or get to use a special plate that's saved for such occasions. Or he may get to choose the evening's menu (within the bounds of good nutrition and affordability).

There are other treats that you can offer as rewards, from ice cream sundaes to inexpensive toys.

I don't mean to suggest that you should bribe your kids to do every little chore. A rewards system like this is applicable for something more than merely doing homework or accomplishing a small assigned task. But if a child shows great improvement in cooperation, or suddenly begins doing his homework on his own without being told to, or undertakes to perform a large task or chore he wasn't asked to do, or helps out with a chore that's out of the ordinary and requires a lot of time or effort, or displays great thoughtfulness in a sticky situation, you can show him you appreciate his efforts or his achievement by rewarding him.

Recognition of efforts is one way of motivating kids. By recognizing their accomplishments, you motivate them to want to try harder the next time. But what about motivating them in advance of an arduous, unpleasant, or simply boring task? Let's look at that old bugaboo, room-cleaning, again. (It may be the cause of more hassles between parents and kids than any other single issue.)

Of course you can simply issue an edict: "Your room needs to be cleaned today. Please do it now." The child will probably argue, or plead to be allowed to do it later. Even when you stick to your guns and insist he go in right now, that doesn't guarantee that the room will get cleaned. He may shuffle things aimlessly around, accomplishing very little. He may uncover a comic book in the clutter and stop to read it. He may simply sit on his bed and sulk over how unfair you are, or how unfair the whole world is.

None of these activities is helping to get his room cleaned.

How can you motivate him to really make an effort and clean it? In part, this depends on knowing what will work best with your child, which we discussed earlier.

- You can stick your head in the door of his room every ten minutes or so, look for signs of progress, praise and encourage him if it looks like he's really getting somewhere with the project, or chastise him if it looks like he's been goofing off or sulking.
- You can remind him that it's a lovely day out, and the sooner he gets his room clean, the sooner he can go out and play.
- You can tell him that if the job isn't done within an hour (or whatever length of time you think is reasonable), he isn't going to be allowed to watch TV tonight.

- You can remind him that the reason his favorite comic book got ruined was because his friend stepped on it, not seeing it under all that stuff on the floor, and that by cleaning his room and keeping it clean, he can avoid such accidents in the future.
- You can point out that when he cleans his room, he might find that missing baseball card he's been looking all over for. It's probably in there among all that mess, and the sooner he gets everything put where it belongs, the sooner he's likely to find the baseball card.
- You can tell him that you won't allow him to have any friends over until he gets his room clean, and if Brian rings the doorbell, you're going to send him away unless that room is in satisfactory shape.
- You can tell him that if, the next time you look in on him, he's not seriously cleaning his room, you're going to turn his stereo off and he'll have to work without the music playing, so he'd better get his butt in gear.
- You can tell him that if he has too many games, toys, or comic books to keep his room clean, you may have to take some of them away from him for a while, or give them away altogether.
- You can tell him that if he cleans his room properly today and keeps it neat for a month, you'll paint the room blue, like he wants.
- You can remind him that everyone has to do things they don't like. You don't like sewing clothes or cleaning house or spending two hours in traffic getting to work and back every day. Daddy doesn't enjoy painting the house or raking the lawn. But you do the things you need to do and so does Daddy, and your child needs to do so, too. Nobody said he has to enjoy cleaning his room. But he has to do it. That's what the world is like, and he'd better get used to it and deal with it. Life isn't all fun.
- You can remind him that, after hassling with you last week and winding up in tears, he finally buckled down to it and got the room clean. Now, he can wind up in an unpleasant scene again, or he can get to work and get the room clean and have it done and behind him. Which does he want? He's already proven—to you and to himself— that he does know how and he can do it when he sets his mind to it. Does he want another unpleasant scene, or does he want to get the chore done and get it over with, so he can do something more fun?

These are some suggestions. You can use whichever works best for your child, or even a combination of two or more. You may even think of one or more others that will work better with your child.

A good corporate executive is a visionary

A good corporate executive can see what the future may be like. First of all, she has a good idea of what her hopes are for the company and how things will be for it in a year, five years, ten, or twenty. And second, she can envision different scenarios, different what-ifs. What if a certain product takes off and sells well; what if the new product that's in development turns out to be a winner; what if the company outgrows its current quarters and has to move to larger ones, either renting a bigger office (or plant) or buying a building of its own.

She can envision the downside, too. What if the country experiences an economic downturn; what if the new product doesn't sell well; what if the suppliers of raw product raise their prices outrageously; what if the union goes out on strike; what if a competitor introduces a cheaper version of a similar product.

Having envisioned all these scenarios, both good and bad, she has contingency plans to deal with each situation. But most of all, having a vision of where the company is headed, she knows what she wants to do, and what she needs to do, to get it to where she wants it to go.

A mom, too, needs to be a visionary. While living day to day is all right on some levels, it also helps to have a long-range vision of what you want for, and expect for, your family in the time ahead. Especially long range. It may be unrealistic to expect your two-year-old to grow up to be a doctor, but it's not unrealistic to assume that he's going to go to college, and to make plans now to help ensure that this happens.

Putting money aside for a college fund from the day the child is born is one step to ensure this. Seeing that he does his homework and studies his textbook is another positive step. Buying him a computer of his own, ensuring that he has a quiet place to study, and helping him when he has trouble with his studies are all positive steps toward getting him into a good college.

If he has trouble doing well in school, there are further steps you can take. Don't just discipline him or chastise him for failing to study. Maybe there's a specific problem. Have you tested him for dyslexia, ADHD, or some other learning disorder? Have you requested a conference with his teacher? Have you hired a tutor who can help bring him up to speed? If you're dealing only with day-to-day situations and not looking ahead, you may see only the poor marks on his report card now and not the possible effects on his future. But if you're envisioning his future, you'll realize that his future in college is being threatened by his poor marks now.

The visionary mom looks ahead, sets her eyes on a goal, then decides what she can do to make the goal a reality. The visionary mom has plans for her family's future, plans for how to make that future happen, and contingency plans for what to do should something go awry.

The visionary mom knows where the family is headed in the year ahead, the next several years, for the duration of her kids' childhood, and even beyond.

A good corporate executive has a knowledge base

A good corporate executive has resources she can draw on for the information she needs to succeed. These may include:

- People inside the company who keep her informed about what's going on within the organization.
- People outside her own company who keep her informed about what's going on in her industry, and in related industries that have an impact on hers.
- Trusted advisers who can give her information about such topics as the many facets of dealing with employees.
- Business publications that keep her informed about the business world at large.
- Industry publications that keep her informed about the specific industry she works in and other industries that impact her business.
- The World Wide Web.
- General reference materials.

A mom needs a knowledge base too. Her sources of info might include:

- Her mother and other relatives who have ever parented a child.
- Her friends who are parents.
- The parents of her kids' friends.
- Books, magazines, and other publications (e.g., newsletters) on parenting.
- Books, magazines, and other publications on other subjects specific to the needs and situations of her family. (These may include publications on any medical condition any of her kids have; on careers moms can engage in from home; on any situation the family finds

itself facing, such as buying a first home, taking an RV vacation, or coping with having three generations under one roof; on raising gerbils, or any hobby one of the kids is interested in; or on most anything else specific to the needs of her family or any of its members.)
- Her pediatrician.
- The school nurse.
- Her kids' teachers (or preschool teachers or day-care providers).
- Her babysitters.
- The neighbors who report that "Jimmy was doing wheelies in the street while he was riding his bike yesterday afternoon."
- The World Wide Web.
- Parenting groups—real world or online—that she belongs to.
- Her local library, not only for the books it has but for any relevant programs it offers.
- Organizations that specialize in a particular problem or situation (whether that's a health situation for a "special needs" kid or one dedicated to a child's hobby or other interest).

A mom makes the best use of all the information at her disposal, but also knows when to ignore that information and go with her instincts, her gut feelings, or her knowledge of her own family and how its individual members may be different from those of the "typical" family, or the family of the person who is advising or informing her. She distills the information she gets from all sources and then decides what is the best thing to do for *her* family, or the individual family member whose situation she is looking for help with.

A good corporate executive is passionate about her job

One of the traits that sets off a really good corporate executive from the others is that she really cares about her job and throws herself into it. She isn't just going through the motions, showing up for the minimum requisite hours, doing what she has to do, and counting the years till her retirement. (She may look ahead to her eventual retirement, but she isn't simply marking time till then; she cares deeply about what she's doing *now*.) The really good corporate executive lives her job. Yes, she has a life outside her job. Everyone needs that balance—outside interests, friends, ways of de-stressing—but her job is seldom far from her mind *because she really cares about it.* At times, when she's far from the office, she'll have a sudden inspiration for how to solve a problem at work. And when she is at work, she is fully involved, because her job isn't just a job to her; it's something she really cares about.

Mothering is probably the hardest job of all and the closest thing to a full-time, 24/7 job there is. Even when you put the kids to bed, you have "one antenna up" to hear if someone is crying, awake and sleepless, having a bad dream, or otherwise in need of attention. Even when the kids are teenagers, reasonably independent, and out for the evening on their own, you worry about car crashes, about whether they'll be home by their curfew, about what they're doing while they're out with their friends and whether they're behaving sensibly.

Is it any wonder motherhood requires a deep commitment beyond what any ordinary job calls for? Is it any wonder mothers, more than almost anyone, are in need of whatever recreational opportunities they can grab to de-stress themselves and relax? Whether it's an hour spent over coffee at a friend's house, a night out at the theater, or simply the relative sanity of the office where Mom works from 9:00 to 5:00, it's a break from the constant pressure and tremendous responsibility that is motherhood.

No wonder moms need a serious commitment to their job of mothering! Mothering is nothing to be undertaken lightly, not a part-time job, and is an occupation that you really need to give your all to. It helps if you care passionately about what you're doing and what results you're producing. You're not raising those kids casually; you have a lot invested in them, and I don't mean the money for Bobby's braces or the cost of setting Suzy's broken arm. I'm talking about the emotional investment in the kids and how they turn out.

I'm talking about nights spent trying to bring Austin's fever down when it spikes at 104 degrees at 3:00 a.m. I'm talking about trying to explain to Zac why Great-grandpa won't be around to take him fishing anymore. Or explaining to seven-year-old Kate that best friends can make up after a fight, and she hasn't necessarily lost Brianna's friendship forever. Or explaining to sixteen-year-old Ellyn that she'll never forget her first love but she really will get over the heartbreak of being dumped. Or waiting to hear from colleges and being more nervous than your daughter is, coaching her for the spelling bee, and telling her that doing her best is all anyone can ask of her, while secretly hoping she goes all the way to the national championships. I'm talking about watching the class play and being more nervous than your son is, exulting that in third grade he isn't playing a tree anymore but has a speaking part, and trying not to shout out his lines from the audience when he forgets them.

This isn't just a job. This isn't just something you do part of the time. And this certainly isn't something you do dispassionately. Your hopes, fears, and dreams are invested in your kids. You care passionately about what happens to them—both now and twenty years from now. You want to see them get good marks on their report cards next week, exhibit signs of greater maturity next year, and enjoy satisfying and reasonably lucrative careers in the more distant future. You take good care of them and shepherd them through life not just because it's your responsibility but because you really *care*.

Mothering is way too tough a job to do halfheartedly. To do a good job of it, and to do it without resentment and without totally losing your mind, you have to be really involved in the process and the outcome. You have to care passionately about your kids, their present-day lives, and their futures.

A good corporate executive learns from her mistakes

Everyone makes mistakes. Mistakes are inevitable from even the most careful, most competent people. But what do you do when you make a mistake? A good corporate executive may well err in judgment. It happens. She may place too much trust in an employee who's not equal to that responsibility, or decide to develop a new product that winds up a failure, or, given two ad campaigns to choose between, she may pick one that proves ineffective, causing sales to stagnate or even plummet. But when she makes a mistake, when she chooses the wrong person to head the new department or selects a logo that turns out to have negative connotations, she recognizes her mistake, she corrects her mistake, and she learns from that mistake.

The lesson may simply be not to make that mistake again, or there may be a larger lesson inherent in the experience, but she assimilates the knowledge gained from recognizing the error, and she puts it to good use.

A mom can do the same. The mistake may be expecting too much of a four-year-old, or introducing too many new foods at one time to a child who's resistant to change, or trusting a teenager to get home by curfew even if the mother isn't waiting up for him to check on his arrival time, or expecting her nine-year-old to be reliable enough to be left home alone for brief periods because the child's older brother was all right when left home alone at age nine. The nature of the mistake isn't important. What's important is: Has the mother learned something from it?

Your kids will often know it when you've made a mistake. You don't need to worry about this, and you don't need to pretend you're perfect. The kids know better—and what's worse, if they do believe you're perfect, they may give up trying to improve themselves, knowing they have no hope of emulating you and reaching your level of perfection. No, if you goof up and they know it, use it as an object lesson in learning from your mistakes. You're human, but you own up to your errors and you correct them, and you expect them to do the same.

This will accomplish two things: it will instill greater confidence and respect for you in your children, and it will serve as a good object lesson.

If a mom expected too much of her four-year-old, does she now realize that, and will she adjust her expectations accordingly? Or will she keep expecting too much of him, keep getting disappointed, and keep expressing that disappointment to him, eroding his self-image? If she tried introducing too many new foods at one time to one of her children, will she keep doing it, hoping that he learns to like some of them (and wailing that he's unwilling to try new things)? Or will she take a slower approach with him, recognizing that this is a child who is resistant to change? And will she extrapolate a greater lesson from that, realizing that other changes in his life, too, need to be introduced slowly, not too many at once? If her teenager breaks curfew when he thinks he can get away with it, will she stay up and wait for him next time? And will she realize that he's at a stage at which if he can get away with something, he will, and so she needs to be wary of more than just curfew violations?

You can't repeat the same mistake and hope that "next time will be better." Yes, eventually the four-year-old will be five and then six and, at some point, able to meet greater expectations. Hopefully the child who's resistant to change will learn to eat some new foods eventually. The teenager will grow more mature and responsible, too, and may eventually respect curfew even when he's not being checked on. *Eventually* you can try again with new responsibilities, new foods, unsupervised curfews. But not for a while. For now, you need to realize that what you tried, what you thought, what you expected was a mistake, an error in judgment.

If you ever allowed your husband to bounce your toddler up and down vigorously just after eating, you (and he) probably realized that was a mistake. The cleanup you had to do imprinted that lesson on you. Learn from your less-graphic mistakes too. Don't repeat them while hoping for a different outcome. Your kids aren't the only ones in the family who need to learn. Motherhood is a continual learning process.

A good corporate executive is skilled at conflict management and resolution

I've heard corporate executives complain that they feel like kindergarten teachers. They might as well substitute "mothers" for "kindergarten teachers." Mothers have to be experts at solving disputes.

Executives are sometimes called on to resolve all manner of conflicts—union versus management, two factions of workers or two mid-level managers who have differing beliefs on the right way to handle a situation, a situation between a lower-level employee and her manager that can't get settled at their level but has to be brought to the higher-ups. In a small company, interpersonal problems between two employees may even fall into the boss's lap to resolve.

A good corporate executive knows how to work to resolve these differences. A good mom, whether faced with internal family conflicts or with conflicts between a family member and someone outside the family, must also be the peace broker. The conflict may simply be between two siblings: "He pushed me." "She pushed me first." It may be a problem one child has with a friend, a problem for which she hopes Mom has an answer. It may be a conflict with a teacher: "Ms. Edwards kept me after class again today for fighting with Sean. But she never keeps Sean after class, and he's the one who always starts it!"

Often a good first step is to get the child to restate the problem: "Belinda won't ever let me use the yellow crayon." Then ask Belinda if this is true and, if it is, what the reason is. If it's not true, why does she think her brother sees it that way? Now you have to be a Solomon and issue an edict that will resolve the conflict—or come up with a solution that will avoid the conflict, such as buying a separate box of crayons for each child.

If the conflict is with someone outside the family, you need to either suggest a way of your child's handling the conflict or step in and mediate the dispute yourself. Deciding when to intervene is a tricky matter. You can't fight all your child's battles for him. This won't help him learn to resolve his own conflicts and to do so peacefully. On the other hand, you can't be too steely or appear indifferent, always insisting, "You need to learn to fight your own battles." There are some conflicts that kids just aren't prepared to handle. How old is the child? How serious is the conflict? Has the child made an effort to solve it on his own? Have you suggested a means of resolving it, which the child already tried to no avail? Maybe it is time for you to step in.

And if the conflict is with a teacher (or other authority figure), the child may feel the situation is hopeless. Adults have all the power. They make all the rules. Sometimes it's very tough to be a kid. And sometimes it helps for you to step in even if you suspect that the teacher is right and you're ultimately going to side with her. If you promise the child you'll "look into it" (not promise to take his side), you can meet with him and his teacher, listen to her version of the dispute, and perhaps explain to the child why, even though it seems unfair, the teacher's position is not unfair. Because you didn't promise to make things right, only to go with him and talk to the teacher, he won't feel you betrayed him when you don't resolve the issue in his favor. He may accept the outcome, or he may still be unhappy, but at least he'll know you were willing to step in and try to help.

A good corporate executive is a decision-maker

A good corporate executive can't be wishy-washy. She has to be able and willing to make decisions, to believe in her convictions, and to be prepared for the occasional wrong decision on her part. Even the best of corporate leaders occasionally make bad decisions. Do you remember the flap over "New Coke" several decades ago? The public roundly rejected the revamped version of Coca-Cola that the company's executives had decided to bring out, and "Classic Coke" made a quick comeback by popular demand. The original formula of Coke wasn't the only thing about the episode that was classic: it was a classic case of bad executive judgment.

Corporate executives know they need to make decisions and to stand by those decisions. A decision may be made based on facts, intuition, or industry information, or a combination of all of these. It may be a decision for which the executive takes several weeks of deliberation and consults with others, or it may be a decision she is called upon to make on the spot, but she needs to exercise her best judgment in any case and not shirk the decision-making process.

Moms, too, need to make decisions. From mundane decisions of what to serve for dinner to larger decisions such as whether to put Becca in private school or public school (a decision Mom will undoubtedly arrive at in concert with her husband, unless she is a single parent), Mom is either the sole decision-maker or one of them. From deciding whether to let Clay have a snack now and risk spoiling his appetite, to deciding whether Pat needs to wear a winter jacket to school or can simply wear a sweater and a windbreaker, to deciding how much money Mom is willing and able to spend on Joshua's birthday party this year, she needs to make decisions all the time.

Some decisions require quick answers: "Mom, can I watch that new TV show?" "Mom, can Jenny sleep over tonight?" "Mom, can I wear my new pants to school today?" Some decisions require much thought, such as what the kids are going to do over summer vacation, whether Sonya and Derek are old enough now to stay home alone in the evening without a babysitter, or when and how to explain menstruation to your daughter, whose breasts are beginning to bud.

But whether a decision is trivial or major, requires a quick answer or much forethought, and is arrived at solo or in concert with your husband, you need to be prepared to make decisions, to stick by them and not waver when the kids don't like what you've decided, and to be ready for the occasional time when a decision backfires on you.

You also need to be prepared to change your mind on occasion.

While you can't be swayed by every argument from the kids ("Jason's mom is letting him have a big party at the arcade with thirty kids. It's not fair that I can only have fifteen kids at the miniature golf course!"), you do need to be open-minded. Being open-minded is not being wishy-washy. If you've reached a good decision that you're comfortable with, stick to it, no matter how much the kids argue and plead. But if circumstances or further facts persuade you that your decision might not be the best one, don't be afraid to change your mind.

Look at the executives who pulled "New Coke" from the market and returned to the "Classic" version!

A good corporate executive can anticipate problems

No one can see every problem coming. We all—corporate executives, parents, people in everyday life—get blindsided sometimes. But some problems can be foreseen. And a problem you've anticipated is a problem you're better prepared to deal with.

What happens when a corporate executive can't authorize merit raises this year because the company has had a bad year? She knows there are going to be some disgruntled employees. Knowing her people, she knows whether anyone is likely to try to stir up unrest among the others. She knows one or more people are likely to resign and find work somewhere else, where the compensation is better and the future looks brighter. And, knowing all this, she can plan for it. She can't anticipate the reactions of every single employee, but she has a good general idea that some people may try to stir up unrest and some people are bound to quit. Knowing what's likely to happen, she can take whatever steps are possible to deal with these situations.

Moms, too, need to be able to anticipate problems and, when possible, take appropriate measures.

Your older child has just taken on a load of new chores and responsibilities within the family. Did you just give this child an increase in allowance as a result, an increase that your younger child didn't get because he hasn't taken on any new chores? You know you're going to get griping and perhaps pleading and cries of "Unfair!" from the younger child. You can anticipate this problem, and, because you see it coming, you can take steps to deal with it.

You can designate the allowance raise as "chore money," making it clear that it's a "merit raise" that simply isn't applicable to the younger child. You can tell the older child that her getting the raise in allowance is conditional on her keeping mum about it to her brother. You can sit the younger brother down and explain to him that his older sister is getting a raise in allowance based on additional chores and that when he reaches her age he can be given a similar group of additional tasks and a commensurate raise in allowance. You may think of yet another way to defuse the situation. The important thing is that you foresee it and are prepared.

Let's take another situation: Jessica wants her friend Erin to sleep over. Erin is a hyper child who'll stay up till all hours, keep Jessica awake and giggling half the night, and will not only prevent Jessica from getting a good night's sleep but will keep the rest of the family awake, too. You know this because she slept over once before. Anticipating the problem, you tell Jessica that you'll let Erin sleep over only on one condition: that they sleep in separate rooms. Erin must sleep in the guest room, not in Jessica's room.

One more example: Your son Aaron doesn't want to go to summer camp. Your husband says money is tight this year, and he's happy to let Aaron spend the summer at home and save you money. But you know Aaron is going to be bored out of his mind and bugging you constantly about it. So you look into local programs for kids and try to find out what's affordable, local, and will let kids register for part of the summer. You check with the town's recreation department, the school's summer fun program, the local Y, and whatever other organizations might offer summer activities for kids. When, inevitably, Aaron starts grousing about being bored, you're ready with a list of alternatives: affordable summer programs that he can join after the summer has already begun.

A good corporate executive communicates well

Unless you are a monk who has taken a vow of silence, communication is key in almost anything you do that involves another person. (And even monks have to let their brethren know that dinner is ready or a storm is brewing or there are visitors in the monastery and extra dinner is needed.) In any event, corporate executives are not monks and have not taken a vow of silence. Neither have mothers—and what a good thing that is!

I'm sure you know that "talking" and "communicating" are not necessarily the same thing. First of all, some talk is meaningless blather that communicates next to nothing. And second, much communication is non-oral or even non-verbal. The executive who sends out a memo is communicating, and so is the executive who claps an employee on the back in a comradely gesture, or with the meaning of "Well done!" or "Congratulations!" without uttering a word.

Communication—*good* communication—is necessary in a variety of situations and for a variety of reasons. I couldn't begin to list them all here; let's look at just a few:

- To elicit cooperation among the ranks.
- To stir up the sales force to excitement over the new product.
- To stir up the workers and increase production.
- To learn the cause of a problem and try to settle it.
- To communicate satisfaction with the job someone is doing.
- To elicit ideas for workplace improvements.
- To establish new or changed policies or rules.

Communication is essential in families, too—and here, too, not all communication is oral or verbal. Two of the most important forms of communication in a family are hugs and kisses, which bear the most important message of all: "I love you." That same message is conveyed in Mom's stroking or tousling her child's hair, patting his shoulder, and many other forms of loving touch.

Though such forms of non-verbal communication as backslapping are more typically offered by dads, some moms use them, too, especially with sons who have reached an age at which they squirm uncomfortably at being kissed. Backslapping also comes in handy to convey "Good job!" or "Well done!"

Putting your arm around your child's shoulder while you correct him conveys the message "I still love you, but you need to understand that you did something wrong."

Even playing "This Little Piggie" with an infant is a form of (partly verbal, partly non-verbal) communication.

Facial expressions communicate your feelings—with or without words. What mother hasn't raised an eyebrow, flashed a scowl, or otherwise silently communicated "Stop that!" to the child who is squirming in church, kicking her brother during a visit to Aunt Rose's house, or belching loudly at the dinner table. And when your child boards the school bus for his first day ever of school, the smile, wave, and kiss you beam at him through the window convey cheerfulness and love, no matter how concerned you each are over the outcome of the day ahead.

You communicate with your tone of voice, too. The words "I have bad news," said somberly, undoubtedly precede legitimately bad news. Said in a lighthearted tone, though, they are almost certainly a tease preceding good news: "The freezer's broken, and you're going to have to finish off all the ice cream before it gets ruined."

And then, of course, there are the words themselves. Moms need to convey everything to their kids, from warnings ("Watch the loose front step. Don't trip") to simple information ("Aunt Julia called. Your cousin Kenny's birthday party is next Saturday"), from education ("No, 'Europe' is spelled with an 'E'") to admonitions ("If you poke your brother again, you're going to your room, and no dessert this evening!").

Good communication elicits information, too. The question "What happened in school today?" is too often met with a non-answer. The good communicator will instead ask, "Tell me about your day in school. Did you have any tests or get any papers back?" followed by, "What grade did you get on your paper?" Other good questions include "Any excitement on the playground today?" "What's the best thing you learned today?" and "Any assemblies or special programs today?"

Skillful questioning can help you get to the bottom of the cause of a fight between siblings (or between one of your kids and a visiting friend, or a child from the neighborhood). Adept questions can also help you find out why your child suddenly professes to hate school, or why he claims not to feel well and to want to stay home from school, when you suspect there's no real physical malady, or why he doesn't want to go to Martin's birthday party

("The last party I went to, there were girls there and they played kissing games. Ugh!").

Good communication means talking *with* your kids, not *at* them. Even when you have to correct their manners or other behavior, a lecture is likely to fall on switched-off ears. Better to fall back on the old standard approach: "How would you feel if Will pushed *you*?" or "Why do you think it's OK for you to pinch Nancy?" or "Did you really expect to bite Pat without Pat doing something to you in return?"

Remember that communicating is about getting your message across. Choose your words well. Choose your other forms of communication too. Don't lecture. Explain. Don't preach. Talk. And don't scream unnecessarily. (Yelling "Watch out!" to the child who's about to step out into a busy street after a lost ball is necessary screaming. Chastising him for a misdeed in a highly raised voice is not.)

A good corporate executive is consistent

As I write this, a friend of mine is in a bind because one of his middle managers has let an employee get away with misdeeds for which his other employees have received reprimands or even been fired. Now the employee who's gotten away with the misdeeds unscathed thinks she's untouchable. Meanwhile the other employees in the department are burning because this one woman has escaped any reprimands or disciplinary action. The middle manager has come to my friend saying that he's lost control of his department and needs help from the top.

It all began with inconsistency.

An executive must treat all employees equally (not identically—they're individuals, who need to be responded to differently—but equally). An executive must be evenhanded in his or her treatment of employees and of similar situations.

An executive should also be consistent in her general demeanor. If she's normally placid, she must make an effort not to blow up on slight provocation just because she's having a bad day. Employees need to be reasonably able to predict her responses to situations. If a particular error or other unfortunate event would normally elicit only a groan and a "Please don't let that happen again," it's unfair and unnerving for her to issue a stern rebuke, a warning of dismissal, or some other reaction far stronger than what the employee could reasonably expect. By the same token, if a particular misdeed or error in judgment would normally incur harsh consequences, letting the employee off with a "slap on the wrist" is likely to raise charges of favoritism.

A mother has to be just as consistent. The mother who is managing her family like a well-run corporate machine knows she has to be just as even-handed in meting out reprimands, corrections, and other justice. The child who complains, "But when Seth stood on the couch and jumped on it, you didn't send him to *his* room!" is within her bounds to complain, unless there are mitigating circumstances. (For example, when Seth did it, it was his first offense. Claudia has been warned three times already. Or Seth is only three years old, but Claudia, at eight, is old enough to know better, and bigger and more likely to cause damage, too.)

As well as being consistent in responding to the misdeeds of different kids, a mom needs to be consistent in responding to the misdeeds of the same child at different times. Does this sound familiar: "Last time I forgot to let the dog out you only scolded me. It's not fair to send me to my room this time"? If the response is cumulative, it *is* fair. If the child keeps forgetting, this is the fourth time in two weeks, and you think something more than a talking-to is called for, progressively sterner measures may be appropriate. But what if the last time he forgot to let the dog out was four months ago, and he received only a scolding? Now four months have elapsed, and he's forgotten again, and this time you've confiscated his favorite video game for a week for punishment. Is that fair? No. Why? Because it's inconsistent. This isn't a case of cumulative response; it's a case of inconsistent response.

Maybe you're having a bad day. Maybe you have a bad headache. Maybe two bill collectors in a row just called. You're only human, and it's certainly understandable if you get irritated a little more easily under the circumstances. But try to rein in your trigger responses and treat your kids with consistency—consistency from one child to the next, consistency from one similar event to the next. (The opposite side of the coin is true, too: if things are going exceptionally well for you, don't let your good mood induce you into letting a child get away with a misdeed that normally would garner a talking-to or a punishment.) And try to keep your overall demeanor as consistent as you can. Don't rain your bad mood down on the kids. It's not fair, it's not easy for them to understand or cope with, and it confuses them.

A good corporate executive knows how to take advantage of possible negative outcomes

What good can come of a negative outcome? Well, for one thing, it can serve as an object lesson. If an employee errs in judgment, and there is a negative outcome, the company head (or department head) can (without demonizing the employee who made the error) use the experience to make a point to the rest of the company, or the rest of the department.

If the employee has only just started down a path that's likely to lead to a negative outcome, the savvy executive can point out the probable negative outcome and suggest that the employee revise her plan or her actions *before* the unhappy consequence is likely to occur.

A mom can do the same. If Noah bounces on his bed and falls off, spraining his wrist or breaking his arm, you can use that experience as a teaching tool, both for Noah, the next time he engages in risky behavior, and for his sister, who might also think bouncing on the bed looks like fun.

If Noah forgets to close the back door every time he goes out into the yard to play, one way to help him remember to close it is to point out a negative outcome that he can relate to. He's hardly likely to be impressed that he's letting the air-conditioning out of the house and driving up the electric bill. But try telling him that if he leaves the back door open, a bee might fly into the house and sting him later on. Now, *that's* a negative outcome he can relate to, and one that might actually result in his remembering to shut the door. If bee stings don't faze him, try telling him the cat might get out and get lost and not come home.

Presenting either of these possibilities to him is more likely to help him remember to close the door than simply reminding him over and over. It's a creative—and effective—use of a possible negative outcome.

A good corporate executive displays confidence in her people

People frequently live up to our expectations of them, whether those expectations are good or bad. A good executive knows that expecting her people to underperform will frequently result in their doing just that—and expecting them to do well will elicit just that sort of positive job performance.

By displaying confidence in them, she achieves three things. First, she gives them a positive work atmosphere, one in which their abilities are trusted and their boss is happy with them. Second, she imbues them with belief in their own abilities. And last, she elicits the sort of good performance that she expects and wants from them.

Moms, too, know that kids often live up to our expectations, positive or negative. If you expect a child to fail, to mess up, or to perform poorly, often he will. There are two explanations for this: because your lack of confidence in him means that he doesn't learn to have confidence in himself, and because he knows you expect him to mess up anyhow, so what's the big deal if he does? Regardless of which reason is the cause, the effect is the same: he underperforms, or performs poorly, at whatever the matter is at hand.

But if you have faith in the child, your faith is contagious and he'll have faith in himself. Because you believe in him, he'll believe he can do whatever it is he's supposed to do, from telling the truth to riding his bicycle safely to learning his multiplication tables. By having confidence in him, you give him more than just the confidence that he can do one task well; you help give him a belief in himself: "I must be a pretty smart kid."

Of course your actions have to be in agreement with your words. It's no use telling him, "I know you can do this task yourself" if you're hovering over him every minute and exhibiting concern, saying, "Do this," "Don't do that," "Do it this way," "Be careful!" "Don't mess up!" You have to match your attitude and actions to your verbal message.

8

EMPLOYEE
DEVELOPMENT

Like the leader of any enterprise—of course, yours is your family—you want to help your people develop to their fullest potential. Any good corporate head would do so for the good of her organization, and hopefully also with the good of each individual employee in mind as well. You, as a mom, have even more incentive to help your people develop as completely as possible; after all, that's a major part of what parenting is all about. Not only will it help your family to work better as a functioning and cohesive unit when your people develop and use their skills, but one of your prime missions is surely to help your people achieve their full potential and develop all their inherent abilities. And this goes not just for educational and career-oriented skills but life skills.

Continuing, then, with the frame of reference we used in the last chapter—the traits of a good corporate executive—how does a good corporate executive help her people develop to their fullest potential?

A good corporate executive recognizes her people's strengths and uses them

A good executive whose administrative assistant is dogged about details will rely heavily on that assistant for help with detail work. A good executive whose head of personnel is amazingly creative and clever and a good writer, too, will either move that person into the advertising or marketing department or, should that not be possible, may invite him or her to sit in on some meetings and brainstorming sessions. A good executive who recognizes that one of her key people can do a good job of handling one of the executive's own functions in the company will delegate that responsibility to this other person, freeing herself up for other tasks and responsibilities.

An *insecure* executive will be afraid to move people around because "that's not the way we always did it." Worse, she won't lay off her own responsibilities on the person who can fulfill them well, because she fears that this other person might eventually take over her job, or because she fears that, if she isn't overworked and hectic, she won't look needed and important.

A mom, too, knows the strengths of those around her and puts them to good use—and that applies to her kids, to her husband, to the larger family, and to the others who interact with the family.

If twelve-year-old daughter Jennifer is good at art, perhaps she can do something decorative to the house (such as painting a picture on the door of the coat closet) that will truly improve the house's appearance while also making Jennifer feel like a proud contributor to the family.

If thirteen-year-old Ryan has a marvelous way with his younger brother, Mom can let Ryan babysit the young boy while she runs to the store unencumbered and gets her shopping done in half the usual time. (Jennifer, at twelve, might seem the more logical babysitter, since babysitting is more commonly a girl's job, but if Ryan is better with his brother, and Mom knows it, she'll be smart to assign the job to Ryan.)

If Jennifer is a good cook for her age or simply enjoys helping in the kitchen, Mom is smart to let Jennifer help in as many ways as possible. Mom gets help and Jennifer learns to cook—a win-win situation.

Knowing her husband's strengths (and weaknesses) is smart, too. Let's suppose her husband is a wonderful baker. She'd do well to let him do at least some of the baking for the family. The kids can learn from that the joy of contributing work to the family, not to mention the fact that gender roles are arbitrary, and men belong in the kitchen, too. And if he's not so handy around the house? She'll set a good example for her kids by not insisting that hubby do all the household repairs just because he's a man. (If he's too lazy to do work around the house, that's a different problem. But if he's genuinely inept, she shouldn't belittle him or insist on his doing home repair chores he's not equipped for. The kids can profit from her example.)

What are the strengths of the extended family? Can Grandma or Grandpa teach the kids how to cook, bake, garden, do woodwork, speak French, take good photographs, or dance? If Mom's smart, she'll encourage the kids to learn all they can from Grandma and Grandpa (or cousin Carl or Aunt Caroline). She'll also let these other relatives contribute to the family if they offer. If Grandma or Aunt Louise knits and offers to make homemade sweaters for the kids, that's great. If cousin Ruth offers to put up Mom's tomatoes in jars or make jam from the abundance of berries in the family's garden, Mom shouldn't demur. She should say "Thank you" and accept. (Mom can always offer for cousin Ruth to keep some of the tomatoes or jam as a thank-you.)

What are the strengths of the other people who populate your family's life? I once knew an aspiring actor who cleaned houses to make money while waiting for his big break. He cleaned my house for me weekly, and I soon learned that, like many actors and actresses, he was reasonably proficient at singing and dancing as well as acting. I asked him if he'd be interested in giving my daughter tap lessons. He was glad of the extra money, which was still much less expensive for me than a regular dancing school would have been, *and* she got one-on-one instruction—and what made the setup even sweeter, I didn't have to chauffeur her to a dance school, as he gave her her lessons right in our house.

If your babysitter is a math whiz, maybe she can help your son with the class he's having problems studying for. If your neighbor is a veteran of the Korean War, maybe he can be a valuable source of information for your daughter's history paper. If your butcher was born in Jamaica, and you're thinking about a family vacation there, I bet he'd be happy to fill you in on the average temperature, the local customs, and the restaurants offering authentic cuisine and frequented not by the tourists but by the locals.

Know the strengths of those people who populate your family's life, and draw on them for all the help you can get.

A good corporate executive recognizes her people's weaknesses and helps them overcome them

Just as a good executive knows her people's strengths, she also knows their weaknesses. And not only does she know what they are; she knows when they are something that can be overcome, and she strives to help her people overcome them. Now, obviously, someone in the art department who suffers from innumeracy is never going to wind up transferring to the accounting department, and a person with no facility for foreign languages is unlikely to learn one in a crash course before an upcoming business trip overseas.

But not all weaknesses stem from inherent inabilities. Some skills and abilities can be acquired. For example, some shy people need only a big dose of self-confidence to blossom. The executive whose shy secretary lacks sufficient belief in herself can, if she cares to be nurturing, help this woman gain greater self-confidence and come out of her shell. The result? Not only has the executive done a kindness for someone, but she may find that she now has in the person of this woman a new sales rep, customer relations rep, or other position. If the secretary is loyal, knowledgeable about the company, and a hard worker, she has great advancement potential. And once she overcomes her shyness, she can readily move up the ladder.

A mom can similarly work to help her people—her kids—overcome their weaknesses. Let's start with the same problem: shyness. If eight-year-old Matt is shy in front of people, Mom will gain little ground by simply urging him to talk to people. But she might try buying him a magic kit. If he grows proficient at performing magic tricks, his desire to show his new-found ability at his magic act may trump his fear of people. Suddenly the boy might blossom, finding courage to perform in front of groups. (Plenty of actors and actresses have started out as shy kids, too. They find that when they take on a role, they transform themselves into the parts they're playing, who are people who aren't shy. As long as they're playing a part, performers can easily step onstage in front of large numbers of people.)

Mom can help her shy or timid kids by giving them lessons in singing, arming them with joke books from which they can develop a stand-up comedy routine, or otherwise helping them become some sort of performers. They needn't aspire to perform professionally; the purpose of this effort isn't to give them careers but to give them confidence. (Though, certainly, many a show business career has been born this way.)

To once again use cooking as an example—it's an important skill and one everyone really should possess to some degree—the mom who's a good executive manager can instill in her kids a love of cooking born of a love of eating good foods, or of being creative, or of being nurturing. There are so many appeals to cooking, many otherwise reluctant kids can be drawn in by one of these methods. So if your kids are old enough to cook but are inept or uninterested in the kitchen, tempt them with the prospect of creating foods to their own liking. If the idea of making something delicious doesn't do it, the opportunity to be creative may. And for some kids, the chance to feed the family with an I-cooked-it-myself creation is all the spur that's needed.

Figure out which aspect will most appeal to *your* kids and you can probably tempt them into learning at least the rudiments of how to cook.

The mom whose kids are lazy, disorganized, unreliable, or surly has a harder time of it ahead of her. But that doesn't make her task any less important. She needs to help those kids lose these negative characteristics and become better citizens of the family and of the world. *How* she can do this is not a question that bears an easy answer. Much depends on the age of the child, among other factors. But her best shot is to try to motivate the child into wanting to change the negative characteristic. You don't have to throw up your hands and say, "Well, that's the way she is." Many traits are changeable—as a good corporate manager knows.

For example, how do you motivate a disorganized child who can never find her homework, her favorite sweater, or where that terrible smell is coming from (the half-eaten chicken wing on the plate under the pile of comic books on the desk)? Likely not by criticizing, lecturing her on the importance of neatness, or threatening punishment if her room isn't clean.

The punishment may be necessary, but even if it is, it's not sufficient by itself. You need to make her *want* to change her ways. A good executive with leadership skills will try to lead that child into *wanting* to be more organized by making organization seem desirable. One too many F's for homework handed in late (because the child couldn't find it in her messy room), one too many bugs in her room (because of that stinky old chicken leg growing moldy under the bed), one too many pieces of clothing that at best are unwearable when she wants to wear them, from having been left crumpled on the floor, or at worst are no longer wearable at all because she spilled ink on them or otherwise permanently messed them up—any of these can be motivation to change.

At that point, you need to strike while the iron is hot. Rather than lecturing (she'll just tune you out), you need to take her side and help her get better organized "so this sort of thing doesn't keep happening." (Put that way, it doesn't come off as a lecture, and she'll be more amenable to listening.) You may need to buy her bins or baskets to organize her stuff in, or shoe trees for all the shoes she just can't keep neat on the closet floor, or you may need to build or buy her some shelves or cabinets, or otherwise help her to be able to be better organized. Labels for noting the contents of cabinets, drawers, bins, and other containers may be helpful, too. But motivating her and then giving her some help will be a far more effective approach than simply lecturing her, scolding her, punishing her, or demanding that she clean her room today, which does nothing toward keeping it neat tomorrow.

Helping a child overcome surliness is more of a challenge, but once again you need to find a way to motivate him instead of merely attempting to correct him through discipline, lecturing, or other negative approaches. One approach is to lead him to an understanding of how his attitude affects other people's feelings toward him. Everyone wants to be liked.

And for the child who lacks sufficient self-confidence, the best approach may be to find one thing she excels at, whether it's a school subject, a hobby or interest, or a personality trait, and work with her at building up that knowledge, skill, or trait till she's filled with pride in herself. At that point, her sense of self-worth will grow and, with a little luck, begin to encompass more than just her pride in her particular skill. Her overall belief in herself may grow.

A good corporate executive listens to complaints with an open mind

Whether the complaint is about management, procedures, rules, fellow employees, or otherwise, a good corporate executive listens to the complaints without a negative mindset. It's very easy for her to get her back up and adopt an adversarial posture, but that doesn't characterize a good executive. A *good* executive knows that sometimes the employees' complaints are legitimate, and that most of the time they are legitimate to the employees, whether or not the executive agrees.

The complaint may be about the people in place on the management level or team. Of course, there has been friction between employers and employees since the first caveman hired a neighbor to help him build wheels for his fellow cave dwellers. The thing an employer needs to remember, though, is that sometimes an employee's grumbling is just that: the complaints of someone who isn't in charge and doesn't like taking orders. But sometimes the employee's complaints are bona fide. Not all bosses wield their power gracefully, and some simply ride roughshod over their underlings.

Do you? Does your husband? Does the babysitter? Do the school teachers or day-care teachers? Does anyone in your kids' lives take too much advantage of his or her position of authority? Give it fair consideration before you dismiss your kids' complaints out of hand. They may have a valid grievance. Does anyone with authority over your kids judge them too harshly, expect too much of them, or discipline them unfairly? Listen with an open mind.

Sometimes the complaints are about rules. Just as a corporate executive must listen to grievances about rules in the workplace, you have to listen to grievances about the rules you've established. Most of the time the kids are just testing your boundaries for them, but sometimes their requests or complaints are justified. You may be too strict, or you may expect too much of them. Sometimes, too, a situation changes and gives rise to the need to reconsider rules or expectations.

The child who's asking for a later bedtime may just want parity with his friend whose bedtime is half an hour later than his own. But it may be that, now that he's nine years old, he's old enough to go to bed half an hour later than his present bedtime. The child who complains about being given too many chores may just be lazy, or trying to get away with doing less. Or he may have so much homework this year that he has no free time once his homework and all those chores are done.

Just as management has to listen to employees gripe about their co-workers, moms similarly have to settle squabbles and disputes between siblings. Unless you're the mother of an "only," you're already all too familiar with the litany of "He pushed me," "She's wearing my sweater," "He ruined my coloring book," and "Make her stop!" Respecting the rights and property of others is a lesson any child needs to learn, but kids with one or more siblings particularly need to learn that lesson and learn it quickly. Surely more fights between siblings arise from some violation of each other's rights or property than any other cause.

And most moms know that although no approach to teaching respect for the rights and property of others is guaranteed, one effective way is to ask, "How would you like it if she wrote all over *your* picture?" or "How do you feel when *he* barges into *your* room when the door is closed?"

A corporate executive who is insecure in her authority will see complaints as challenges to that authority and move to squelch them with no regard for their validity. A mom who's insecure, or one who's overly authoritarian, will similarly see complaints as such challenges. But employees work more willingly, and harder, for a management they perceive as sympathetic and understanding. And kids who perceive their "management"— their parents—as fair-minded and open-minded will be more cooperative and tractable. On the other hand, though, if they feel that you never listen to their complaints or take them seriously, they may feel less willing to listen to you either.

If you've worked your way up in the corporate ranks and have had superiors of both types, which were you more willing to work hard for, listen to the requests of, and generally be cooperative with: the boss who listened to your gripes or the one who dismissed them out of hand?

A good corporate executive sets boundaries

An executive needs to set various sorts of boundaries:

- Boundaries for the behavior of employees.
- Boundaries for expenses.
- Boundaries for the number of new products or services the company will try to launch in a given year.
- Perhaps even boundaries for her own accessibility to the public or to her employees. (This last one doesn't mean she needs to make herself inaccessible, but she might set hours during which she's "in" to people who want to see her, or do it only by appointment, rather than letting anyone come in anytime and disrupt her concentration and work flow.)

The executive mom sets boundaries, too:

- Boundaries for the behavior she'll tolerate from her kids.
- Boundaries for expenses.
- Rules for everyday behavior and for unusual circumstances.
- Limits of excessive or hazardous horseplay, backtalk, squabbling, lack of manners, untidiness, and other negative behaviors that she'll put up with.
- Limits to the number of sweets, carbonated drinks, salty snacks, and other non-healthful foods she'll allow per child per day.
- Limits to how much food a child may eat, how soon before dinner a child may take even a healthy snack, and other food-related issues.
- Limits to the number of interruptions she'll tolerate when she's trying to talk to someone, balance the checkbook, use the bathroom, or take a nap.
- Limits to how messy she'll allow a child's room to get before she mandates a cleanup.
- Limits to the type of language she finds acceptable (this may pertain to insults as well as to cussing or "gross" language) and to the tones of voice she finds acceptable as well as the vocal volume ("Don't screech!" "Don't yell in the house!") she will tolerate.

- Limits to the number of friends she will permit a child to have over as guests at one time.
- Limits to the behavior of her teenager in matters regarding persons of the opposite sex.
- Limits to driving privileges for a teenager.
- Limits to what clothing she deems appropriate—based either on appearance, on the weather, or on suitability for the occasion on which it's being worn.

In short, Mom needs to set a lot of boundaries. Without having it spelled out for them, either verbally or in some sort of employees' handbook, the personnel of a firm can't know what work is expected of them, how much goofing off is acceptable (coffee breaks, personal phone calls, Web surfing or reading personal e-mail on company time, or arriving habitually late), what rules and standards and dress code they must follow, and whether it's acceptable to answer questions about the company if approached by reporters or other writers. By the same token, you can't expect your kids to know what their boundaries are unless you spell them out, and you can't expect them to observe and honor those boundaries unless you enforce them.

If you do choose to ignore a boundary for once and break your own rule, or allow the kids to do so, it's best if you tell them, "Just this once we'll ___," and it's even better if you can give them the reason for bending the rule. This way they'll understand that they're not simply "getting away with" something due to laxity on your part, nor are you changing the rules.

Kids need the structure of boundaries, even if you're not a strict, totally by-the-book executive, even if you're the sort who tends to "wing it" as you go through life. Kids need to know what is expected of them, what behaviors will not be tolerated, what rules they're required to obey. Not only does this clarify for them what's permissible and what isn't, but it prepares them for the world at large, where there are rules they will be expected to follow and expectations they will be asked to live up to, in school, later on at work, and as citizens of the nation and the world. From "Don't interrupt" (at least, not needlessly) to "Don't litter," some of the rules are the same for adults as for kids.

A good corporate executive fosters creativity

A good executive prizes creativity from all her people, not just those who work in areas that are supposed to be creative (e.g., advertising, art, public relations). The employee who thinks creatively may come up with an idea for a new product or service, for a new feature for an existing product, for a new solution to a thorny problem, for a clever way around a corporate obstacle, for a way to handle an internal dilemma or one with a client or supplier, for an innovative way to save money. In short, there are no limits to the types of useful, helpful, productive, stress-relieving, or budget-easing ideas an employee might have if he is encouraged to be creative and to share his ideas with management.

A mom has twice as many reasons to encourage and foster creativity. Not only will it help in family situations, but it's a good trait for her kids to have as people.

Creativity within the family is a good thing because, to come back to our discussion of kids coming up with solutions to problems, creative thinkers can often think of new and different solutions. Sometimes we're so tied to doing things the same old way, or to a mindset that tells us we're simply stuck with a problem with no solution, that we fail to see a creative way out, a clever way around the problem. But if your kids can "cut through the underbrush" and get to the heart of the dilemma, then think of a clever, creative way around it, isn't that a good thing for the whole family?

And creativity is an asset in other areas, too, not just in problem-solving. Creative thinking can help in planning out a family vacation, a birthday party, even a menu for a special evening. Creativity is useful when a child has to write a thank-you note. Creativity is an asset in some specific games and just in playing in general. The creative child can amuse himself a lot better than can the child with little imagination.

The child with little imagination needs structure to have fun. He needs a boxed game, or equipment (even if it's simply a basketball) and a set of rules for how to play with that equipment, or at least someone instructing him in what to play and how to play it. The creative child, given two sticks, might invent a stick-throwing game, or use the sticks as drumsticks, or pretend they're people and invent a conversation between the two of them, or go look for more sticks and try to build a structure with them. But he's far less likely to sit there and complain, "I'm bored. There's nothing to do."

And creative children are more likely to grow up to be creative adults, a trait to be prized no matter what walk of life the child follows when he grows up. Not only are creative adults more likely to be writers, artists, musicians, actors, and others in the arts, but creativity is prized among scientists, people in the advertising or marketing industries, people whose careers bring them in close contact with many other people, and many other careers. Creative teachers can better enhance a curriculum and bring it to life for their students. And, to come back to where this particular item started, creative employees in all industries can often come up with solutions for situations, dilemmas, obstacles, or problems in their workplaces. (And those who rise to the top are particularly likely to be creative.)

So be a good executive mom and foster creativity in your children. You'll be helping them both now and in the future.

A good corporate executive encourages her people to work independently

Though working in an office (or any sort of company) requires a team effort and a good team spirit, there is much merit to being able to work independently. The worker with the proper amount of independence is not a loose cannon, running off and doing his own thing and going against the grain of what the company deems appropriate, or against the current efforts or goals of the company. But he does not need to be directed in every move he makes. He has the initiative to tackle projects without needing help and direction at every turn, without needing to be "baby talked" through every step of the project, and without being told what to do at all times. If this is a project for which he does need aid or input, he finds his own source of info or assembles his own team.

And his manager, or the top executive, encourages him in his independence. As long as he is not going off half-cocked and tackling inappropriate projects, or treading on someone else's toes, or working at cross-purposes to the company's goals or principles, the independent worker is a joy to the manager who doesn't have to "hold his hand" through every step of every project, tell him what to do step by step, or tell him when he needs to accomplish every aspect of his area of responsibility.

Very often these independent workers are the same ones who exhibit the leadership traits we just discussed above. But not every employee who can work independently can also lead others well. Fortunately, however, it is not necessary to be a leader in order to work independently; it is only necessary to "lead oneself."

And working independently is a great trait in kids, too. The child who works independently can clean up his room without Mom having to sit there and direct, "Now put all your blocks away. And now the books. Now pick up those clothes from the floor. Are they clean? Put them where they belong. That one's dirty? It goes in the hamper," and so on. The child who works independently will do his homework with minimal prompting and will ask for help only when there's some part of the homework that genuinely buffaloes him.

The child who works independently also plays independently. He won't need Mom to make suggestions because "I'm bored. There's nothing to do." He won't need Mom to play with him most of the time, either. True, if he wants to play Old Maid, he's going to need an opponent, and if he has no sibling, or she's not available, and he doesn't have a friend over, then Mom (or Dad) will be "elected." But if he's coloring, he won't keep asking Mom, "What color should I make his shirt?" And if he's building a fort out of the throw pillows, he won't keep asking Mom for help. And unless he needs a partner or opponent for a specific game, he won't keep asking Mom to play with him.

Mom should encourage her kids to play and work (such as at room-cleaning) independently when possible. Of course she'll want to spend some time playing with even the most independent of young kids, but she should also encourage her kids toward independence in play and work if they don't seem so inclined on their own. If a child working on a coloring book asks, "What color should I make his shirt?" Mom can deflect the decision back to the child with, "What color would you like it to be?" or "What color do you think would look good?"

And what of the child with the messy room (and isn't that virtually every kid?!) who elicits his mom's help in cleaning with "I don't know what to do first"? If the child is four years old, it's probably appropriate for Mom to give some help or guidance. But by the time the child is old enough to read and write, he's also old enough to clean his room without being guided every step of the way. His mom can give him more help at first, then slowly wean him from needing as much direction.

For a few times, she can make a list of what he should do and the order he should do it in:

PUT AWAY BLOCKS
PUT AWAY BOOKS
PUT CLEAN CLOTHES AWAY
PUT DIRTY CLOTHES IN HAMPER
PUT MARBLES IN CONTAINER
PICK UP ALL BASEBALL CARDS AND PUT IN DRAWER

And so on. When she's done this for him a few times, she can suggest the next time that he make his own list and bring it to her for her to look over.

When he does, she can make suggestions for adding to or improving the items on the list or putting them in a better order. After she's "proofread" his list a few times, he should be able to make a list and follow it without her supervision. Now all she should need to do is to check the room over when he thinks he's finished and call his attention to things he's missed.

The child who wants help at every turn with his homework is likely either insecure about his ability to follow directions or is simply trying to get Mom to do his homework for him. If she stays firm about not doing the work for him, only helping him understand what's too difficult for him, he'll learn after a while not to hope she'll do his work. And as for his difficulty in following directions, her best plan is to ask him what the assignment says and what he thinks it means. This way, instead of spoon-feeding him the process, she's helping him to learn to understand it on his own. (If he consistently doesn't understand the instructions correctly, there may be an underlying problem that's greater than his simply lacking independence. He could possibly have a vision problem, be dyslexic, have a learning disability, or in some other way have a genuine impairment.)

But Mom should encourage whatever degree of independence is appropriate to the child's age, whether it's "Play by yourself for ten minutes while I finish what I'm doing, and then I'll be in and play with you for a while," or "Now, you know what the weather is. It's the same temperature as yesterday, and it's sunny out. *You* tell *me* what you should wear today."

Don't worry. The child won't interpret it as your ignoring or rejecting him, nor are you encouraging him to be so independent that he won't need you anymore. You're simply encouraging him to be an independent person, capable of playing on his own, working on his own, and making his own decisions. And these are good traits at any age, and both at home and in the workplace. So be a good corporate manager in working to help your kids toward being independent.

A good corporate executive strives to develop her people's skills and talents

The corporate executive who wants to make the best use of the people who work for her will strive to develop those people as best she can. This includes bringing out their abilities and talents to the greatest degree possible. Naturally, the more developed their skills and talents are, the more useful they are to their company. This applies both to those skills and talents that pertain specifically to their areas of responsibility and those that don't now but might come in handy in the future. After all, a promotion (or even a lateral move) might place an employee in a position where a skill or talent formerly irrelevant to his job might unexpectedly become a great corporate asset.

How does a good executive develop her people's abilities? In several ways. For one, she may send them to training classes in which they can better develop a skill for which they have shown some proficiency. Or if it is not appropriate or feasible for the company to send them to training on company time or at company expense, she may encourage them to do so on their own time and at their own expense. She can point out, if it's true, that the incurred expense will pay off in the long run if a move up the ladder is the likely result.

Sometimes, the promotion precedes the acquisition of skills. If an executive sees promise in an employee, she may promote him to a higher level, to a position for which he does not have all the needed knowledge but in which she believes he can quickly get up to speed once he gets his feet wet. If there are others in the department from whom he can learn the necessary skills, she may advance him up the ladder, or even move him laterally to a position in which he has better prospects for future advancement than he does in his present position, and better prospects for being a greater asset to the company.

Sometimes, too, an executive will undertake to mentor an employee personally, helping him to better develop his innate abilities and showing him certain skills that will be particularly useful in his field. If she cannot personally mentor him, whether due to time constraints or for other reasons, she may arrange for some other person with the needed knowledge to be the employee's mentor.

A mom, too, needs to instill and develop good skills and good talents in her kids. She, too, can point her people—the kids—in the direction of appropriate classes or programs. These may be after-school classes in dance, voice, instruments, art, drama, puppetry, creative writing, or some other field of the arts. These may be computer classes, an educational science club, or a group such as FFA (Future Farmers of America), which helps kids develop skills needed for their presumed future careers. She may also try to enroll them in regular schools with enriched programs, in which they can enhance their innate talents or develop their interests in the arts, a particular science, or whatever field they show promise in.

As well, she can try to share with them whatever special knowledge she has herself. Whether Mom is or ever was an accountant, a chef, a ballerina, a doctor, a filmmaker, or a writer, or has knowledge and skills from some other field, she can share her knowledge of her field with her kids, especially with one who shows promise in, or interest in, that field.

She can also find a mentor for each of her kids. If Suzanne is interested in charcoal drawing or auto mechanics, and Mom has a friend who's proficient in the medium of charcoal or the skill of car repair, she can ask her friend to take Suzanne under her wing and help her make the most of her talent or interest.

Just in her own attitude, Mom can make a difference, too. Some moms would discourage Suzanne's interest in auto repair ("That's for boys!" or "That's not a very prestigious career" or "That doesn't pay as well as being a doctor" or "That's hard work and dirty and uncomfortable" or even just "It's a phase; you'll grow out of it"). Rather than discourage her child, if Mom sees that Suzanne has a sincere interest in the field (and I am not talking now about a four-year-old's fascination but an older child's real interest), Mom should encourage Suzanne, whether or not it's the field Mom would have chosen for her.

And if it doesn't turn out to be a lifelong interest? I have a friend who for a while was interested in auto mechanics and actually worked in that field. Eventually she switched careers and became a teacher, but she remained able to do much of the work on her own car, saving plenty of money. Even when she had to take it in to the shop, for some reason such as that it needed to be put on a lift, she never got ripped off by a dishonest repair garage.

Encourage your child in her field of interest, whether it's the one you would choose for her or not. Even if her pursuit of drumming in a garage rock band doesn't lead to an eventual career in music, and fame and fortune, it will offer her happiness right now. And it may offer her a very pleasurable hobby later on.

But what's more, it will lead to her performing in public now, which not only may help her overcome any shyness and give her greater self-confidence but will help her get over any fear of appearing in an onstage situation in public. I teach a course in public speaking, and most of my students are people who need to speak before groups in the course of their work but freeze up at the prospect. Many of these are men and women who address groups as small as ten or twenty people; few of them are public speakers who need to address audiences of a hundred or any number close to it. I'm sure that if they'd been part of garage bands or drama groups as kids, they wouldn't now be so terrified of public speaking as to need to take a course in addressing the public, when for them "the public" is really just a group of ten or twenty people from work, not a large group of total strangers.

So, you see, the talents and abilities you encourage in your kids can have benefits beyond the obvious. If they take drama lessons, for example, not only will they have fun performing now, and perhaps prepare for a future on the stage, but this can even prepare them for a life in the business world. Your kids will get used to appearing in public, and leading corporate meetings or group discussions or whatever their future careers will demand of them will be far less scary for them.

And here's something else to think about: if you denigrate your child's interests, he will feel that his mother never had faith in him, and it will undermine his own self-confidence. By encouraging his interests and talents, you build up his belief in himself. Even if he never follows, as a career path, the interest that grabbed him at age ten or fourteen or sixteen, your belief in him and his dreams will encourage him to follow his future dreams, whatever they may be, and to have faith in himself and his abilities, because *you* had faith in him and his abilities.

A good corporate executive strives to develop the character of each of her people

A good character is surely a necessary attribute in any employee, any member of a team or representative of a firm. From diligence to honesty, from cooperation to trustworthiness, the virtues that together make for good character are highly prized in an employee, and a good corporate executive will do what she can to instill in her people the traits that make them more valuable to the organization.

She will praise an employee's existing good character. She will encourage better character in someone who shows promise but lags a little in exhibiting the degree of good character that might be more desirable. And she will hold up as a good example an employee who exhibits good character, for the other employees to profit from that person's example. She knows that honing her people's characters is valuable not only for them but for the organization as a whole.

It is quite the same for a mom. Mom needs to encourage her children to have good character, to be honest and diligent and trustworthy and cooperative and reliable and straightforward and all the other attributes that make for an honorable person of good character. And a mom can encourage her children in many of the same ways that a corporate manager encourages her people.

Whatever reward systems you have in place for recognizing your child's achievements in other areas—such as cooperation, room-cleaning, or not fighting with a sibling—can be put into play to reward instances of good character as well. Whether your reward is simply the verbal recognition and praise that good behavior deserves or something more tangible, from a gold star to an ice cream or a gift, let the child know you appreciate notable instances of good character.

Did your son tell the truth at a time when a lie would have been more convenient and easy to get away with? Praise and possibly reward him. Did your daughter voluntarily confess to a misdeed without being accused of it or questioned about it first? Praise and possibly reward her. The reward doesn't need to be something expensive or extravagant. It can be some special time spent with you, perhaps an excursion to one of the child's favorite places, or even to someplace that's special to *you*, that you want to share with your child.

Unfortunately for many employees, they often don't get rewarded for doing a particularly good job, landing a difficult account, coming up with a time-saving or money-saving innovation, or just steadily doing a good, reliable job week in and week out. Fortunately, at least some employees get bonuses for such things, and merit raises are more common. I'm not suggesting you give your child a "merit raise" in allowance for honesty, but there are plenty of other ways to reward her—some of them methods that don't cost a penny.

Children need some sort of reward as incentive even more than adult employees do. At their age, kids still haven't accepted the need to do things "because you're supposed to" or "because you need to" as readily as adults have.

Of course, not all rewards are tangible; a good boss knows the benefits of praise and acknowledgment, and so does a good mom. Verbal recognition is sometimes enough of a reward, both for an employee and for a child.

And if your child exhibited less than wonderful character in some way? Let him know you're disappointed in him. Certainly if the transgression is a serious one, some sort of disciplinary measure may be in order, but often a heartfelt talk is what's really called for. Explain why it's important to tell the truth, or why it's important not to steal, or why he should always respect the rights of others—whatever is applicable to the situation. Make sure he understands why this rule is important. It's not just "a rule." There's a reason for it. Let him know you're disappointed in him, but let him know, too, that you still love him, and that you have confidence he can do better in the future.

Holding up good examples is another valuable method, as well. How do you do that? There are various ways, but pointing out that "Your friend Pete would never do such a thing" is probably not among the best of them.

Don't set him in competition with another child his age, or with a sibling he sees as a rival. Rather, choose someone older he looks up to.

If yours is a family in which there is a much older sibling, whom the child looks up to and admires, *then* holding up a sibling as a comparison may be a valuable lesson. The child's father or grandfather, grandmother, or favorite other relative can also be used as an example. It's good if you can tell the child a specific story about that relative that illustrates his displaying the character trait you want the child to develop. "Did I ever tell you the story about Uncle Eddy and the bicycle?"

Books about people with admirable character traits are useful teaching tools as well. The books may be biographies of real people or fictional books whose protagonists display—or learn—the character traits you want to inculcate in your child. (If we're talking about a pre-reader, read the book aloud to the child, as long as the vocabulary level is appropriate for him to understand the book.)

Try to help the child see that there are two reasons for having a good character: she will feel better about herself, and others will like and respect and trust her more as well.

A good corporate executive grooms the leaders of tomorrow

A good corporate executive knows she won't be at the top of the organization forever. She may retire, or she may jump ship to another company, but sooner or later she will leave the helm of the company, and someone else will be needed to take her place—perhaps someone from within her own organization. In that case, if it is someone she trained and not an outsider who's been brought in, she can know that she is leaving the company in capable hands. She can know she is leaving the company she built up and led to success in the hands of someone she trained, who she can hope will continue to lead the organization in the direction she would like to see it continue. So it is in her best interests to groom her successor. In addition, some of the people below her will go on to leadership positions in other companies.

An insecure executive may fear that grooming her people for leadership may result in one or more of them challenging her authority. But a confident executive will know that she still holds the reins. She is still securely at the top. What's more, she knows that every future leader she trains will remember her and the lessons she taught that future leader. She is leaving a legacy behind, a legacy of knowledge and instruction and good example that remains within each of these future leaders.

And isn't that exactly what a mom does? Right now you are the executive of your family, but one day your children will have families of their own. Whether you are raising sons or daughters, one day they will likely be parents—executives of their own families. Surely you want them to be the best parents they can be. Well, start training them now in all the things they need to know and be and do to attain their full potential as parents. And one of these traits they need is the quality of leadership.

Yes, there is much more to being a good leader than simply having good leadership qualities, but let's start by examining that one. A good leader has the courage of her convictions, yet is willing to admit that she might on occasion be wrong, or that someone else might have a plan that's superior to hers. A good leader has faith in her own decisions, yet is willing to let others question her without perceiving it as a threat. Still, if she is questioned, explains herself, and fails to persuade the questioner, she doesn't falter in her conviction if she knows her course of action is correct.

A good leader is persuasive. She doesn't rule by brute force or bullying. She rules because she exudes confidence and inspires confidence in her troops. And she rules because she makes wise decisions, which bear out the value of following her lead.

She also rules evenhandedly and fairly, not as a despot who makes arbitrary decisions that aren't grounded in fairness.

And, by good example, she inspires those beneath her to follow in her footsteps.

When your daughter Debbie has her friend Maryellen over for a play date, and she says, "Let's play house," she's taking the lead in a very small way. If Maryellen says, "No, I want to play Barbies," how does Debbie respond? If she says, "It's my house! We'll play what I want!" she's being a despot.

If you overhear this exchange, what do you do to help Debbie overcome her despotic tendencies (which of course are natural for children to exhibit)? Do you say, "Let Maryellen choose the game. She's the guest"? That's teaching Debbie good manners but not leadership. It's better to say, "Why don't you take turns? You can play house for a while, and then you can play Barbies." That's an improvement.

If Debbie is old enough to reason well, though, you can try adding, "What do you like about playing house? If you explain it to Maryellen, maybe she'll see it your way." And of course, maybe Maryellen won't. Maybe she's stubbornly set on playing Barbies, and that's that. But if Debbie attempts to persuade Maryellen by explaining why she wants to play house, she's exhibiting a leadership quality. Granted, her early efforts at explaining are likely to be ineffective and unsuccessful, but now you're teaching her a better approach to getting her way than bullying, crying, or threatening ("If you don't play house, I won't be your friend anymore"). And she just might succeed in her efforts—if not this time, then maybe next time.

And if she fails? Then she can fall back to the compromise position: "We can play Barbies for a while and house for a while." Leaders have to learn the art of compromise, so you're still teaching her a leadership skill.

Good leaders don't bully, so by teaching your child not to bully, again you're teaching her good leadership. (Teaching leadership is as much about teaching what not to do as about teaching what to do.) Good leaders don't give in too easily; a good leader isn't a pushover. But good leaders aren't stubborn either. They know they can't always have their way. A good leader knows which issues are worth fighting about and which ones to let go.

Of course, not every child has leadership potential, nor can the world be full of all leaders. If everyone in the world were a leader, whom would they lead? The world needs some followers, too. If you try to mold your child into a leader, but it seems obvious that he isn't one, if he always lets his sibling or his friends lead the way, if he's content to let others make decisions for him, accept that you have a follower. Don't try to mold him into something he isn't. Just teach him to stand up for his rights and not be a pushover.

A story I remember reading a couple of decades ago concerns a father who helped his daughter write her college application. One question, which the parent was supposed to fill out, asked if his child was a good leader. The father answered truthfully that he was sorry to say his daughter didn't exhibit much leadership potential, though she was a very good follower. They sent off the application, with the father feeling good about his honesty yet regretful about its possible consequences. To his amazement, his daughter was accepted to the college. A note with the acceptance pointed out that the college had had some astronomical number of applications from students, each of whom, with the exception of this man's daughter, was alleged to demonstrate marvelous leadership skills, and "with that many leaders, what we really need now is followers."

Part of grooming the leaders of tomorrow is encouraging leadership skills. A good executive doesn't look at her employees only as cogs in the machinery, subservient people who are there to follow directions and take orders and perform the work she needs done. She knows that among them are the leaders of tomorrow.

Among the people in any given department may be one who may well become the next head of that department when the current department head moves on or retires. Someone, somewhere—perhaps even some employee right within the company—will have to take over the leadership of the entire company when the current executive retires (or moves on to a better position elsewhere). And if she truly cares about the company, she will start grooming someone now who can be her right-hand man or woman in the interim and a good fit as the new CEO or president when this current executive moves on or retires.

An insecure executive is afraid to encourage leadership skills. She fears someone under her outshining her and stealing her thunder (and the employees' respect for her, and perhaps even her position). Lacking sufficient self-confidence, she doesn't want to let the employees demonstrate their leadership capabilities. She'd rather be the boss of a herd of sheep. But that isn't healthy for her company.

Moms, too, are sometimes afraid to encourage leadership skills. There are various reasons. Some moms are afraid that independent kids with good leadership skills won't listen to Mom as readily. Some moms see the child who can take charge of her younger brother or sister, or a household situation, as a competitor with Mom herself and her authority. Some moms, who have an unhealthy need to be needed, see an independent child with leadership skills as someone who may soon grow autonomous and not need Mom anymore.

Some moms are just uncertain how to engender leadership skills in their kids. Of course, if you have several kids, you can encourage older Jessica to keep younger Ryan and Morgan amused and find creative ways to do it, to keep an eye out that they don't get into any kind of danger, and be responsible for them, more so than just amusing them. Even if your child is an only, consider telling him that you'd like for the family to do something together on Sunday evening, and you'd like him to plan the evening. Give him some guidelines, such as "Nothing that costs over fifteen dollars," "Something we can all do at home with the TV off," or "One activity that's educational and one that's totally fun." If you have a child of nine or ten or older, you can ask her or him to plan an interesting, well-balanced menu for three nights of the next week, subject to your approval.

By delegating tasks that require taking the initiative and making decisions, just as corporate managers do with their people, you give your kids a chance to practice devising ideas, making decisions, leading others, and perhaps persuading those others that this plan is a good plan and worth following—all aspects of leadership that they need to master in order to hone their leadership skills.

The corporate executive who sees in a shy violet the potential to be more of a leader will encourage her to challenge herself and rise above her insecurities or her lack of experience. The executive may task this woman with leading a meeting, complete with a presentation on a current project or problem. And the woman, though terrified and sure she'll fail, will take up the task because the order came from the top. Though fearful and uncertain, she may well succeed, even if it's only a qualified success. This will encourage her to believe in her abilities and impel her to try again more willingly the next time the boss gives her such a task, or may even impel her to volunteer next time. One such challenge can even be a major transforming experience.

The mom who mothers in the corporate mold will take her cue from the executive who's molding the leaders of tomorrow. This mom knows that her children need to develop leadership skills to use in their future lives. They are better prepared both for their eventual likely entry into the business world and for taking charge of their own lives as well. This mom also knows that developing leadership skills in her kids helps them to be more involved participants in the family right now.

How? In a number of ways. The child with leadership skills is more likely to take the initiative in getting things done helpfully around the house. If Mom is struggling with a cranky two-year-old, the eight-year-old with leadership skills might say, "Mom, I'll set the table for you while you get Jeffrey calmed down." If the situation is that Mom feels a migraine coming on, her son with leadership skills might organize his younger sister into an impromptu dish-washing brigade. Though it's not normally their chore to do the dishes, he might say, "Hey, Patty! Let's you and me do the dishes so Mom doesn't have to deal with them."

A twelve-year-old child with leadership skills, on a grocery-shopping trip with Mom, might say, "Let's have a barbecue Sunday. My friend Mikey's coming over, and Bethany's friend Alison is coming over, too. If Dad grills out, you won't have to cook for all those extra people. And with paper plates, there's fewer dishes to wash. How about we get some chicken and some ribs?" He's identified a situation: two extra people are coming for dinner on Sunday. He's recognized that this means more cooking for Mom and more dishes to do, too. He's come up with a solution: let Dad grill out, which creates less work for Mom, then serve the food on paper plates, which cuts down on the dishes. And he's even taken the initiative in planning out part of the menu: chicken and ribs for the meat dish.

An older sibling with leadership skills can take charge of a younger brother or sister and help ease Mom's burden. I am thinking here not so much of the thirteen-year-old who babysits her nine-year-old brother so Mom and Dad can have a night out. Mainly I am thinking of the child who shepherds her or his younger sibling through the day, not just getting him juice when he's thirsty if he's too young to get it himself, or keeping him occupied, but really taking charge. I am thinking of the child who helps his or her younger sibling get dressed, if the child is young enough to need such help, who takes the younger child to the kitchen and makes breakfast for him, if the older sibling is old enough to do so, who finds an activity for the younger sibling and even gets involved in it if need be.

If the younger child is a pre-reader, the older child may offer to read a book to him. If the younger child wants to watch TV, the older child will find a suitable program for him. If the younger child wants to go outdoors, the older child will say, "Mom, I'm taking Cody out into the backyard," and will make sure Cody is properly dressed for the weather, helping him into his jacket if such help is necessary.

If the younger child is jiggling and holding himself, the older child will urge him to use the bathroom. If the younger child says he's hungry, and the older child knows it's nearly lunchtime, she will urge him to have patience and tell him it's nearly time when he can eat lunch. If he says his stomach hurts, she'll suggest he lie down, then report the situation to Mom.

The child with leadership skills is the one who organizes the Father's Day surprise for Dad, the party for Mom's birthday, the family choir at Christmastime—all of them good contributions to the moments that make up family life now and make for wonderful memories later.

Leadership skills involve not only initiative and thinking but also good people skills—something we all surely want our kids to have in both business situations and social ones. After all, being a good leader means more than just telling someone what to do. You have to tell that person in such a way that he is willing to listen and follow. (Bossiness is *not* good leadership!)

So encourage leadership skills in your kids. Don't worry that they might become too independent. You can always rein them in if they spread their wings too wide, either for their own safety or for your authority. But if they don't develop leadership skills early on, it's harder to instill those skills later. And leadership skills are a valuable trait in your kids, not only later, when these skills will stand them in good stead in their careers, but right now, when they'll be of help to *you*.

A good corporate executive gets to know her people—and what makes each one tick

Though the executive of a huge company can't possibly know every one of the thousands of people who work there, she *can* know the key people. And the executive of a much smaller company can know *all* her people. By "knowing" I mean more than just recognizing their faces and knowing their names. She should know what motivates these people, how best to relate to them, and how to get the most out of them. She should know which ones work best when left alone to accomplish an objective, and which ones work best when given guidance, or feedback, or encouragement, or all of these, whether they're working on a special project or involved in day-to-day operations.

A good corporate executive knows who is best motivated by the "carrot" approach (the promise of rewards) and who best responds to the "stick" approach (urging, or even threatening, if need be), and who needs both the carrot and the stick. She also recognizes who among her people is a self-starter who needs neither carrot nor stick but simply needs to be told what needs to be done. (She will still see to it that this person is properly acknowledged at the successful completion of a task, whether the acknowledgment is in the form of a bonus or a raise, a promotion, recognition at a company awards banquet, or simply praise and thanks for a job well done.)

A mom, too, knows her "people"—her kids—and what makes them tick. She knows each child and whether that child takes the initiative on a project (whether we're talking about room-cleaning, homework, or helping a younger sibling get dressed) or needs to be urged to get active on a project.

Does your child take pride in setting the table without being told to? Then don't tell her; let her undertake to do it on her own, then praise her and thank her. It's time enough to tell her if this happens to be the evening when it slips her mind, and dinner is nearly ready. Is she the sort who needs to be reminded to set the table? You have two choices: you can verbally prompt her every evening at the appropriate time, or you can set up a chores chart that details what each child's responsibilities are. (For some kids that's not enough; some kids will still need the verbal prompt.)

Does this sound like you? "Hilary, why do I need to tell you to set the table? You know you're supposed to set the table every evening before dinner. I shouldn't have to remind you! You're old enough to know that 6:30 is dinnertime and that by 6:15 you need to start setting the table!"

It comes back to knowing your people. Your "Hilary, why do I need to tell you to set the table?" was a rhetorical question, not a literal one. But take it literally: why *do* you need to tell her? You need to tell her because that's what works best for her. She's not a self-starter. Not all kids—and not all adults—are. She's a child who needs to be prompted. Perhaps in time she'll grow into taking the initiative, remembering that it's time to set the table and she needs to do it, and will do it without reminders. Maybe next year. But for now, if you know whom you're dealing with and how she operates, you can minimize a lot of friction.

Change your expectations of her. Accept that she is not a self-starter. Does she set the table when asked? Does she do a good job of it? Does she do it without a lot of grumbling or resistance? Be happy with that.

Don't say, "Your sister, Maggie, does her chores without being told." Maggie is a different person, perhaps one who strives to please you and needs the praise that comes with taking the initiative. In fact, Hilary may be the more independent of the two! It's possible that Maggie is diligent because she has a strong need for the praise she will garner by accomplishing her chores without being told, while Hilary is more internally secure and doesn't have the same need for frequent praise.

Do you know what makes Hilary tick and what makes Maggie tick? Think about it.

And while you're thinking about what makes them tick, think about how to best utilize this knowledge to get each of them to do what's needed. Elicit cooperation from Maggie by giving her the praise she craves. Elicit cooperation from Hilary by giving her the reminders she requires. Don't expect Hilary to emulate Maggie; they're two different people with different responses, different emotional needs, and different intellectual capabilities.

The same thing is true in disciplinary matters. Maggie's eagerness to please you probably means that the most effective response to a transgression on her part is for you to express disappointment in her. Telling her she's let you down will probably be more effective than confining her to her room, or depriving her of an excursion to the movies. She craves your approbation. The words "Maggie, I'm disappointed in you" will have a stronger effect on her than will docking her allowance.

Hilary, on the other hand, probably won't be as bothered by a simple talking-to that expresses disappointment. Of course you need to tell her that you disapprove of what she's done (or failed to do). And if you think she doesn't understand why it was wrong to borrow her sister's sweater without asking, or to hit her brother back after he hit her first, you need to tell her and make it clear. But under some circumstances, especially for serious misdeeds or repeats of misdeeds that she's been chastised for previously, something more than simply a verbal reprimand may be in order. You may need to confine her to her room or otherwise punish her.

And there again, it helps to "know your people." If Hilary is an avid reader, confining her to her room—where she can sit and read for hours—may not be an effective punishment. Better to deprive her of a cherished privilege. Save the room confinement for the child who likes to spend all her free time outdoors with her friends.

Now, what about homework? How do you get a child to do it and, in the case of older kids, to really study and not just do the minimum work required? Again, you need to know the child and what motivates him. Let's start with *when* the homework should be done. Some kids need the break from school and really work better if they have an hour of free time first before delving into homework. Others will do better if they get the home-work done first thing, so they get it off their shoulders. Some kids need the discipline of sitting down and finishing it all at one time. Others have a short attention span and need to break up their homework into segments: Math homework now, then a break for a snack, and then social studies, and another break, and then English homework.

How do you motivate the kids to get their homework done? Some kids are good students or simply conscientious and will do their homework with a minimum of prodding. Some kids hate homework so much, or are so indif-ferent about school, that nothing but parental insistence will work, and you'll need to review the homework each night to be sure that it's all getting done. Some need to be given the "carrot" approach—a reminder that straight A's (or pulling marks up to B's) may be attainable if they do their work. Others need the "stick"—a reminder that if the homework isn't done, there will be no TV that evening. (For a teenager, the "carrot" might be a reminder that good homework leads to good grades, and good grades lead to a better chance of acceptance at the college of the child's choice.) Some kids need to let off steam for an hour by playing outside, or they'll never settle down to do their home-work. Others need to be told, "If you want to play outside, you have to finish your homework. The sooner you get it done, the sooner you can go out."

Know your people.

A good corporate executive encourages her people to succeed

A good corporate executive wants to see the people in her organization do well, especially within the framework of her company, though she knows their success might lead them to better-paying positions in other companies. She does her best to encourage them to do their best, she gives them whatever materials or help they need to do a better job and be successful, and she congratulates them on a job well done, even congratulating them when their good performance lands them a job at some other company.

A mother, too, knows that her children's success includes eventually achieving independence and going out on their own. But in the meanwhile, she encourages them to succeed at schoolwork, in their clubs or after-school groups or other hobbies, and in their personal lives. Their friendships may mean that the family is not the sole focus of their lives. Their membership in Scouts or band or the youth group of their church or synagogue may mean that they look up to a Scout leader, band leader, or youth group leader whom they revere. Their schoolwork may take precedence over chores at home. But Mom encourages her kids to do their best and succeed at what they do, even though that success will eventually lead them to college, independence, and being out on their own.

Mom gives her kids whatever aid she can to help them achieve success now and an ever greater measure of independence both now and in the future. Whether she helps her son write an essay, shows her daughter which reference books contain the information she needs to complete a homework assignment, hires a tutor to help her son in a subject he's not doing well in, helps her daughter overcome shyness to be a social success, enrolls her son in band (and puts up with the wailing of an ill-played clarinet every afternoon), or drives her daughter and the daughter's whole soccer team to practice, Mom gives of herself in any and every way she can to help her kids achieve both success and, in ever greater measure, independence. And when the kids no longer rely on Mom or need her for everything, she doesn't wail or feel neglected; she congratulates them on having achieved this state and congratulates herself on a job well done.

Mom wants her kids to succeed. She wants them to succeed not only in getting along with her, their dad, and their siblings, and in meeting their parents' expectations, but in school, in after-school activities, in their friendships and other relationships (e.g., getting along with classmates and with teachers), and later, as they mature, in their relationships with their boyfriends or girlfriends and, eventually, in college, in work, and in a relationship with a spouse or significant other. The mom who is secure in her position in life does not begrudge her children their success outside the family, a success that may take them outside the bosom of the family. Instead, she cheers them on. Not only is she happy for them, but she knows that their success means she has done her job well.

A good corporate executive corrects her people when they make a mistake—and then moves past it

Assuredly a mother is a teacher. So is an executive. When someone in a corporate organization makes an error of some sort, he or she needs to be corrected. When one of your children makes a mistake, he or she needs to be corrected as well.

A good corporate executive corrects her people's mistakes, primarily with the good of the organization in mind. If the employee takes correction well, he will learn from the experience and from the executive's correction, and, depending on the nature of the mistake, the lesson may be one that makes him a better person as well as a better worker.

Almost as important as issuing the correction, however, is knowing when to consider the lesson delivered and move on to other subjects. The executive needs to correct the employee. She doesn't want him repeating the mistake, and he may not have recognized the error on his own. Or he may realize now that he goofed up but not have a clear idea of what would be a better course of action to have taken. But having once pointed out his mistake to him, and having suggested a better way to handle that situation next time, the executive needs to drop the subject and move on. Overstating her case and hammering at the employee is a wonderful way to incite resentment in him, and if he's feeling resentful, he isn't going to absorb the lesson very well.

Moms need to follow the same playbook. If a child makes a mistake, be it in manners, in behavior, in judgment, or in any other area, certainly Mom needs to correct him. While the corporate executive's primary motivation in correcting an employee is the good of the organization, Mom is looking out for more than just the good of the family. She is also fulfilling her role as teacher to her kids. So she can't leave the mistake uncorrected. But she too needs to recognize that once her point is made, she needs to let the subject drop.

We've all heard mothers berate and belittle their kids. Which of us hasn't cringed on hearing a mother rail at a child, "Can't you do anything right?" or "How could you do something so stupid?" Certainly that isn't the way to correct a mistake! Making the child feel bad about himself isn't the best way to correct him and will do damage to his self-image as well.

Instead, help him to see that he has not done the best possible thing under the circumstances. Tell him what would be better.

And, if he doesn't understand why, explain it to him. Kids often don't understand the reasons behind rules that are very obvious to the rest of us. You may think it's enough to say, "Don't chew with your mouth open," but unless you've explained to your child (probably several times, so the message sinks in: "It's gross and yucky-looking for the other people around you. Don't do that to us"), he isn't going to understand *why* he shouldn't chew with his mouth open. And the lesson will be much better received and remembered if the child understands the reason behind it. (Yes, he may deliberately chew with his mouth open after that specifically to gross out his sister, but that's a different type of situation, although also one that needs correction.)

But once you've gotten your message across, drop it. Nobody likes to be verbally "beaten over the head." Harping on a subject doesn't elicit a positive response in anyone, adult or child. And no child likes to feel that he'll be reminded forever of every transgression or error. So once you've made your point, move on. You'll get much better results.

A good corporate executive fosters corporate harmony and good interrelationship attitudes

A good corporate executive knows that workers who get along well together will work better together. A workplace filled with squabbling is a workplace in which the employees expend their energies and thoughts in all the wrong directions. A workplace that runs harmoniously is not only one in which the employees don't expend their energies on fighting but one in which they will cooperate, help each other, and work more harmoniously for the good of the company.

A mom, too, knows that kids who get along well together make for a smoother-running family. Some sibling squabbling and rivalry is inevitable, but life doesn't have to be a constant battle. If the older child can be made to feel partly responsible for the younger one, not only will Mom's life be easier with less to do, but the older child will assume the big brother/protector or big sister/protector role and have a better attitude toward the younger sibling. And if the younger child looks up to the older child, that, too, will ensure greater peace and accord.

So Mom needs to work to foster these attitudes, as well as fostering greater cooperation, understanding, and tolerance between the two. It's understandable that the older sibling will resent it when the younger sibling gets away with some form of bad behavior because "He's too young to know better." And it's understandable that the younger sibling will resent it when the older sibling gets some privilege the younger one doesn't have, because "She's old enough to stay up later." A certain amount of friction is inevitable—though, as we discussed earlier, Mom can foresee it and plan for how to combat it.

But nobody wants to live in a war zone—not Mom and, believe it or not, not the kids who are feuding either. They may prefer fighting with each other to simply accepting what they view as an inequity. But if Mom takes steps to defuse the situation by getting at the root cause, instead of just breaking up each individual fight, there will be far less discord.

The family that lives in harmony has less strife, less anger, more cooperation, more helpfulness, and makes for a much nicer home to live in.

A good corporate executive knows how to use incentives and rewards, and when not to

We've already discussed the use of incentives and rewards. Now let's talk about when *not* to use them.

The executive who rewards her workers for everything positive they do will soon find them motivated only by the expectation of a reward. Not because they're there to work and are supposed to go above and beyond sometimes. Not because finding a way to cut costs is good for the company, and what's good for the company is ultimately good for them. Not because signing a new account helps guarantee the company will remain in business and able to pay workers' salaries. Only because they want to get something for *themselves*.

A savvy executive will know when to utilize a tangible reward to award an achieving employee, when to merely give him a verbal accolade, and when to say nothing, do nothing, and simply treat his achievement as part of doing his job.

A mom needs to recognize the same set of circumstances. Rewarding kids for everything good they do sets up unrealistic expectations—both of what they can expect from the family, and what they can expect from the larger world out there. I can't give you a set of guidelines to follow as to what specific acts deserve tangible rewards, which ones deserve praise, and which should simply be expected of the child, but here are a few suggestions:

- The first time a child does something well, or makes a good effort— the first time he makes his own bed, cleans his own room, or uses the potty, for example—praise him. For a few times thereafter, thank him. After that, expect it of him and don't make a big deal of it.

- If a child does something above and beyond what's expected of her, such as feeding her young brother breakfast for the first time, because you're busy trying to deal with a stopped-up toilet, or such as raking the lawn without being asked, and without it being her usual chore, just because she felt like being helpful, praise and thank her, but don't give her a tangible reward.
- If she displays good character, such as by bringing home a wallet she found in the street and handing it to you with the suggestion that you turn it in to the police so its owner can get it back, praise her for her honesty and thoughtfulness, but again, she shouldn't expect a tangible reward. (If the owner of the wallet wants to reward her, though, then let her keep that reward or, if it's more than just a few dollars, put it in her college fund.)

While tangible rewards have their place, kids shouldn't expect a tangible reward just for doing homework or chores, for being extra-helpful, or for everyday kindnesses. They need to learn to do such things as homework and chores because they're expected, and to be helpful and perform kindnesses to make other people happy and perhaps to feel good about themselves. Praise and thanks will reinforce this positive feeling and are sufficient reward most of the time.

If you lead your child to expect a tangible reward for every accomplishment or good deed, you're not preparing her for the real world out there, or for the business world, which she's likely to find herself in as an adult.

9

CHOOSING THE
LEADERSHIP STYLE
THAT WORKS BEST
FOR YOU

Successful corporate CEOs are not all cut from the same cloth. And there is no one right way to be a CEO of a family. In fact, a mom will probably need to change her style as her kids grow, not to mention making subtle changes from one child to the next.

Some CEOs micro-manage. Micro-management is generally not a good leadership style, but if it's the only executive leadership style you're comfortable with, then go for it. This chapter is not about changing your leadership style to conform to someone's ideal of the best way to lead a family; it's about choosing the style that's best for you.

Which personalities are the ones that are best with a micro-managing style? They include:

- The person who's very detail-oriented and needs to oversee all those details herself.

- The person who's very control-minded and needs to be in total control of all situations at all times.
- The person who's very distrustful and needs to oversee everything that's being done by those under her and take charge of every last detail.

This mom is very controlling, takes charge of every last detail, always chooses the clothes her child will wear the next day, has a long set of rules that she lives by and another long set of rules that she expects the kids to live by, and oversees every aspect of her kids' lives.

Sometimes it's not the manager but those being managed who demand this style of leadership:

- Infants certainly need to be micro-managed.
- Certain older children who lack initiative need to be micro-managed.
- Certain older children who are not trustworthy need to be micro-managed.

At the other end of the spectrum is the mom who gives her kids total latitude, who is so laid-back that she's reminiscent of the hippie mothers of the late 1960s and early 1970s. These moms lay down very few rules, giving their kids a great degree of latitude and self-determination. They believe that for a child to learn to be independent, to function on his or her own and be self-reliant, self-directing, and self-sufficient, he or she needs to be almost totally self-determining.

This mom doesn't tell her kids that bedtime is 9:30; she expects them to know when they're tired and go to bed on their own. But if they don't, she simply sees that they go to bed when they're ready. She tells her kids to go to bed when she sees them falling asleep while reading or watching TV, or she picks them up when they fall asleep in the living room and carries them to their beds. She reasons that when they're tired, they'll go to bed, or fall asleep where they are.

This mom is also more laid-back about eating. She may allow the kids to get their own snacks at an early age and trust them to eat what their bodies need, whether or not it's a nutritionally approved well-balanced diet, and she may serve meals on a more haphazard schedule. Dinner may be at 4:30 on Tuesday night and 8:30 on Wednesday night. If at 6:30 her son says he's hungry, and she knows dinner is a couple of hours off yet, she'll say, "There's a chicken leg, some yogurt, and some cheese in the fridge. You can find something to eat. Dinner won't be for a couple of hours." Note that she's directing him toward healthy eating. She's not just letting him gorge on candy. But she's casual and laid-back about routines. Her style is to see that the kids have their needs met as dictated by their bodies, not by her rules.

In fact, many kids brought up under such a system of leadership really do learn independence and self-reliance at an early age, but that's *not* to say it works for everyone—not for every child, and not for every mother.

And then there's the middle road: the mother who neither micro-manages nor lets her kids self-determine. She keeps her hand on most aspects of her kids' lives, but she gives them a little leeway. She practices what was my mother's favorite byword: moderation. Of course this style of mothering encompasses a broad range, from mothers who fall just short of micro-managing to mothers who fall just short of the self-determination style. Most moms fall somewhere within this middle ground.

But there are subcategories of mothering styles too. There is the "organizational mother," who does everything by chart. Her children's chores are posted on a bulletin board, whether they are daily chores, weekly chores, or rotating chores. That bulletin board is likely to be pretty crowded, as it probably also contains her menus for at least a week in advance, planned out and posted for her to refer to. She probably has more than one Things to Do list and may even create Things to Do lists for her kids as well. She may also have a chart in each child's room on which the child can check off each day's required accomplishments ("brush teeth," "comb hair," "dirty clothes in hamper," "make bed," and so on). As well, she may have a chart of the child's attitude and other attributes, such as "cooperative," "thoughtful," "polite," "pleasant," with spaces for check marks or gold stars for each day or each week.

This type of mother is very organized and seldom forgets to return library books or videotapes on time, doesn't forget when it's her turn to provide the snacks for Scouts, rarely has to make unexpected runs to the grocery store for items she's forgotten or run out of or suddenly decided she wants, and generally runs a pretty tight ship. She organizes her errand runs for maximum efficiency, getting the most errands done in the least time in the most practical order. The downside is that she's more easily flummoxed when circumstances disrupt her good organization and she's required to deviate from her menu plan, her Things to Do list, or any of her other planning.

The "by the seat of the pants" mother is more inclined to wing it. She's a spontaneous person and may not know what she's cooking for dinner till she opens the fridge to see what's inside, decides what she has on hand that goes with the main course she's settled on, and makes sure she has all the necessary ingredients for the recipes she's just settled on. She is as likely to assign a chore to her kids on the spur of the moment as to have it be a regularly scheduled occurrence. ("Pam, honey, please wash the dishes tonight. Your brother has a report due, and I need to help him with it, so you're 'It.'") This mother makes more last-minute trips to the supermarket or convenience store, is more likely to make other stops spontaneously (such as stopping at the video store to rent a movie as long as she's passing within a block of the place), and often doesn't know what she's going to do with the kids over the weekend till Saturday morning rolls around.

This type of mother is more relaxed and easygoing. Life with her is more likely to be spontaneous and fun for the kids. On the other hand, of course, she's obviously not as well organized, is more likely to forget that she promised to bake thirty-five cupcakes for Friday morning, may decide to make stir-fry for dinner only to realize she's out of cooking oil, and probably buys more gallons of gas per week for the family van because she doesn't organize her errands for maximum efficiency.

The "prompting" mother tries to get her kids to do the right thing by asking questions: "Do you think your room is neat enough that you can find anything you want in there?" "Don't you think you ought to get ready for bed now if you have a big test in school tomorrow?" "What do you think you should wear to school? The forecast is for a chance of rain, with temperatures in the 60s, but it's only 43 now." "How are you going to smooth things over with Beth after the argument in school yesterday?" "What do you want to say to Grandma before she leaves on her vacation?" She tries to elicit from the kids the response that she wants, but she wants the kids to think things through for themselves and feel that they came up with the answers on their own.

Of course, since a mother's leadership style is as relevant to her child's personality as it is to her own, a mother may find that she's directing one child's life one way and another child's life another way. Some kids need to be micro-managed, whether or not that's the style of leadership most natural to or comfortable for the mother. And other kids will do only what they're told to when they're micro-managed, but they'll take the initiative and clean their rooms, do their chores without being pushed, and even do extra chores, when they're left alone to be responsible for themselves.

If your present style of management isn't effective, or isn't successful with one of your children in particular, consider changing your style. Think corporate. Don't just be a parent; be a manager, and decide which management style will work best for you and your kids.

Too, a mom's style may change from her first child to her second, and on beyond that, if she has more than two. Many mothers raise their first children more by the book and their second children more by the seat of the pants. Their leadership styles, too, tend to be more relaxed with the second child; with the first child, they tend to be more directive. And if there are more than two kids, the mom's leadership style may shift even further.

A friend of mine, oldest of six siblings, recently commented to me that he and the sister, who is the youngest of the six, had compared notes a few months ago about their mom and the way she had raised each of them. The mother's attitude, approach, leadership style, and overall parenting style had changed so radically from when she reared my friend to when this sister came along that the two of them, having this recent discussion, wound up saying to each other, "You didn't have the same mom I had."

10

WHEN IT JUST
ISN'T WORKING

If you read the business section of your newspaper, you've read the stories: stories of well-qualified business executives whose companies nonetheless experience rocky years; stories of executives who are capable and able and well versed in labor relations, whose employees nonetheless go out on strike; stories of executives who are known as visionaries, who nonetheless fail to see that the new product, on which the company is pinning so many hopes, has "DUD" written all over it.

It's not that these CEOs are inept. It's not even that they're underqualified in a particular aspect of their jobs. Sometimes the outcome of a project, the relationship with a particular employee (or with all of them), or the attempt to keep expenses within the corporate budget just doesn't work out, through no fault of the executive's.

And sometimes a mom finds that some aspect of family life isn't working out, despite her best efforts. She's attempting to teach manners to Davy the same way she did to Aaron, but what worked with Aaron so nicely just isn't giving good results with Davy at all. She's being patient and loving yet firm with Amy, but despite her best efforts to understand the girl, Amy is sullen, resentful, spiteful, and rude. And neither warmth and affection nor the withholding of privileges is having any effect.

What to do?

Sometimes a change in parenting style, or in specific tactics, helps. Sometimes it's simply a case of the fact that what worked with Aaron won't work with Davy because they're different personalities and require different approaches.

Sometimes it's a case in which Mom is working at cross-purposes with Dad, or isn't getting the backup from him that she should. If Dad says, of Davy's manners, "He's only four. He'll learn. Give him time," or "Boys will be boys," Davy is going to think that it's all right to be unmannerly.

Sometimes it's necessary to call in an "outside consultant." In the case of a corporate executive, this can be a very expensive proposition, and the consultants a mom may need to call in are often pricey as well, though not all are. It depends in part on what the child's problems are.

If the problems are behavioral and nothing you try is working, it may be that the only help you need is from your mother. Sometimes a child who won't behave for Mom will behave for Grandma. Sometimes, too, though you think you've tried everything, your own mom may be able to make a suggestion for an approach you haven't tried that will be effective.

If Grandma isn't around, someone else may fill the bill—an older person the child looks up to and will listen to, or else someone who can make a suggestion to you for a more effective approach in handling the problem.

But the "consultant" your situation requires may need to be a paid professional—a counselor or therapist or other behavior specialist who can work with the child, or with the whole family, to resolve the situation. The important thing for you to bear in mind is that needing to call in outside help is not an indictment of your parenting ability. The best of CEOs sometimes need outside help, especially with a particularly tough situation, and so do the best of parents, sometimes. So if your family is strained because of a situation you can't resolve with your child, whether it's defiance, bad attitude, extreme rudeness, or some other problem, consider the possibility that this is a problem beyond the means of what's reasonable to expect yourself to be able to handle. Consider the possibility that it's time to call in a consultant.

Professional experts come in handy for other types of problems, too. Sometimes the child who doesn't obey has a hearing problem and actually didn't hear what you told her. Sometimes the child who refuses to do his homework has a learning disability and is simply overwhelmed. Sometimes the child who seems overly rambunctious is not exhibiting misbehavior but rather the symptoms of ADHD. Your problem with the child may require the assistance of a doctor, a trained audiologist, or some other professional.

There are also children who simply can't be led to proper behavior through the usual means. They are out-of-control young kids who grow up to become "wild" teens, who sneak out of the house, steal the family car, and get into all manner of trouble. You may be an exemplary parent, evenhanded and firm, loving and yet no pushover, with a husband who co-parents well enough to be a role model for all other dads, and yet your child is a problem. You may have taken the child to a psychologist years ago, read every book you could find on the subject of "tough love," and yet the child is incorrigible.

You need to recognize that the problem is not your fault. You may need to put this child in a foster home or other setting away from your home, no matter how difficult it is to take this step. You may need to do this not only for your own sanity and to preserve your marriage, but because, in some cases, your home and your person may be in danger, and in many cases, your other child or children are being adversely impacted.

Some employees simply can't be led or handled, no matter how skilled their department heads or the head of the company may be. These employees simply will not work well, or are disruptive, or foment unrest needlessly among the other employees, or are dishonest, and no amount of skillful managing or caring conferences can bring them around. Similarly, some kids are a problem no matter how good a mom's (and dad's) parenting skills are. If you have a child like that, accept that it's not your fault, that the problem lies within the child and not with a lack in your parenting skills, and call in an outside expert.

It's not an indictment of your abilities. And acknowledging that you need help with the problem is not an admission of failure. In fact, it's an acknowledgment of your professionalism to know when you need the help of an expert.

No one can know everything. No one is able to do everything, not even the most adept of executives. That's why good executives, and good mothers, recognize when it's time to call in an outside expert—and do it.

11

FAMILY MEETINGS, BOARDROOM STYLE

Just as executives have board meetings, managerial meetings, and staff meetings at which everyone is present, families can have semiformal meetings too. In fact, there are plenty of families that call "family meetings" when there's a specific topic to be covered, such as:

- Vacation plans.
- A forthcoming move, or other major change in the family's living circumstances (e.g., a grandparent or other relative who is moving into the house).
- A new baby on the way.
- A new job for Mom or Dad—especially one that will create a change in the family's routine.
- A change in financial circumstances that necessitates cutbacks.
- A discipline problem.
- A reassignment of regular chores.
- A decision to begin holding fire drills or other disaster drills for the family.
- A dispute between siblings that needs a parental resolution.

- Some other situation that requires the undivided attention of the entire family at a time when they're not trying to eat dinner, not rushing to get to homework (or a television program, or to the three friends who are waiting outside for them to come out and shoot hoops), not distracted by the six o'clock news on the TV in the background, not in any other way distracted.

But why wait for a problem or other situation that calls for a family meeting? Why not schedule regular family meetings—just as many companies schedule staff meetings for every Monday morning at 9:00, or every Friday afternoon at 3:00? Why not plan to meet as a family at a regular time, whether that's weekly or monthly or at some other interval that works for your family's needs?

Sunday evenings are a good time for family meetings as a general rule, but if that's not best for your family, choose the time that's best for you. Your family may find that Saturday mornings, or Sunday mornings, or even Tuesday evenings are the best time for your family meetings. Make a plan now—for every Saturday morning, or the first Sunday evening of the month, or alternate Tuesday evenings—and schedule your meetings accordingly.

Make it a time when no one has a conflict. Attendance is mandatory, so pick a day and an hour when nobody—parent or child—has a work conflict, school conflict, organizational conflict, or other conflict. And pick a time when social commitments are unlikely. (This effectively rules out Saturday evenings, for example.) If yours is a church-going family, you can plan your meeting for Sunday mornings immediately before services, or immediately after. Again, you can schedule your meetings for every Sunday, every other Sunday, the first Sunday of every month, or whatever works for your family's needs. But the point isn't *when* you schedule the meeting; the point is *that* you schedule the meeting.

What's the agenda for your family meetings?

- Setting family goals. If there is something you're trying to accomplish as a family, some goal you're trying to reach *en masse*, here is the opportunity to discuss it, from growing a family garden to compiling a family scrapbook to reaching out to the relatives with whom you have tenuous connections at best to saving a thousand dollars for a family trip to the Alaskan wilds.
- Airing family problems, whether they're problems the parents have with the kids, grievances the kids have with the parents, problems

between siblings, or problems with some member of the extended family.

- Announcing family situations, whether it's Dad's cutback at work or Mom's promotion and the impact this will have on the family (less time to spend with the family; less money available for non-essentials), Grandpa's diagnosis of Alzheimer's and what that means, Lianne's acceptance on the cheerleading squad, or any other family situations.

- Discussing allowances or other monies earned by the kids: an across-the-board raise for everyone due to everyone being a year older, or being an active participant in family chores, or due to Dad's getting a raise at work; a new structure for calculating allowance or chore monies earned.

- Discussing such situations as whether the kids believe they're old enough to be left on their own in the evening without a sitter.

- Discussing chores. Does Maureen think her chores are too many, given the amount of homework she has to do now that she's in junior high school? Does Mom think Paul should undertake more chores, now that he's ten years old? Does Dawn think she has an unfair number of chores compared with Matt? Does Pat think he should be getting a larger allowance now that he's doing more chores?

Are there other situations or topics for discussion? Both you and the kids can bring them to the table for conversation. The Family Council is a good place for airing questions, problems, grievances.

Whatever the situation, the Family Council (or whatever name you call it by) is the place to bring up grievances, questions, announcements, and other discussions, just as in a board meeting or staff meeting in a corporation. And, just as in a corporate meeting, a lot can get accomplished in a meeting at which everyone is present, everyone participates, everyone is free to air his or her thoughts or grievances, and everyone gets to hear the head honchos (that's you and your husband) speak.

12

ALL WORK AND NO PLAY MAKE MOM A BURNT-OUT EXECUTIVE

The best and busiest of executives take time off for themselves. You can, too. Whether you relax for five minutes or two weeks or somewhere in between, you not only deserve to take breaks, you *need* them. Don't begrudge yourself the time; think of it as a necessity. By relaxing and refreshing yourself, you help yourself to be better prepared for dealing with whatever mothering throws at you. And I'm sure you know by now that it's easier to deal with anything from sick kids to teething infants, from lost library books to crushed teenage hearts, from all-out sibling warfare to having to cover for a sick carpool mom at the last minute, if you're rested and refreshed.

There's a reason so many executives are golfers. They take time off—often not just on weekends but during a workday—to grab some R&R. (They also get into the office at 7:00 a.m. when necessary—just like you, who are "on the job" at all hours.) So please accept the fact that, far from indulging yourself, far from being selfish, you're helping your family when you recharge your batteries by taking a break, whether it's ten uninterrupted minutes in a bubble bath or a week spent in a bed and breakfast off in the countryside somewhere, with just you and your husband, and nobody screaming for "Mommmmm!!!"

Once you accept the fact that not only do you deserve a break but your kids deserve a rested and relaxed mom, the next thing you need to do is arrange for some time to yourself. If all your kids are in school or day care, and you're not working full-time, getting some alone time (or time alone with your husband, your best friend, your mother, or another companion of your choice) should be relatively easy. If you have one or more kids at home during the day, or you work full-time, arranging this is going to require a little more effort.

But it's *not* impossible. And it *is* worth it.

Depending what your plans are, you may want time during the day or during the evening or sometime on a weekend. You probably know what your options are for coverage for the kids, but just in case there's one you haven't thought of, here are some ideas:

- Hire a sitter—possibly one who will watch the kids at a location other than your house, if you want to spend your R&R time at home.
- Offer to trade with another mom. You can watch each other's kids on a regular or irregular or as-needed basis, to give each other a break.
- Make arrangements for each of your kids to spend the night or afternoon at a friend's house.
- Ask Grandma—your mom or mother-in-law—to take the kids for an hour, an afternoon, or overnight.
- Look into a Saturday afternoon program for kids that doesn't require one of their parents to be present, whether it's offered by the local Y, your church or synagogue, a crafts studio, a preschool that also offers such other programs as after-care, day camp, and weekend programs, or any other responsible local entity that offers a fun activity for kids. You not only can have your alone time, but you can know that the kids are having fun at the same time. Depending on who's offering the program, it may consist of gymnastics, athletics, arts and crafts, music, movies, religious instruction, a trip to an arcade. I've even heard of an organization that offers a "birthday party" on weekends, complete with ice cream, cake, soda, games, and goody bags to bring home—everything except a birthday boy or birthday girl, so there's no present to buy, though of course there's a fee to participate.
- Ask your older child (if he or she is old enough) to look after the younger one for ten minutes, or half an hour, while you grab a much-needed break.

- Take a vacation day or "personal day" off from work at a time when the kids are in school or day care and you can have the day to yourself.
- Make a deal with your husband that you'll watch the kids for three hours (or some other length of time of mutual agreeability) while he goes off and does something just for fun, if he'll do the same for you.

Now, how are you going to spend your time?

- If you've got only five or ten minutes, go soak in a bubble bath or do something enjoyable and relaxing like listening to your favorite song while you read a story in a magazine and drink a nice hot cup of coffee or tea. (You can combine all that with the bubble bath, too, if you want!) And never mind that you had a shower just three hours ago; this bubble bath is for relaxation, not cleanliness. In fact, you don't even need to use the soap at all!
- Are you a gardener who truly enjoys puttering in your greenery? Go spend some time in your yard or among your potted plants.
- Want to do something physical to work the stress out of yourself? Go bowling, go to the gym, ride your bike (or rent one), go for a swim, or take a brisk walk.
- Too tired to do something physical? Lie down and do absolutely nothing. Daydream, or simply let your mind wander. Nap if you're sleepy, or just lie there exulting in the fact that the kids are out of the house and nobody's going to be yelling for you, fighting with a sibling, or forcing you up from your well-deserved sloth to investigate the cause of that crashing noise.
- Go shopping. You can even go to an antiques store, free of the worry that two-year-old hands might break something valuable.
- Treat yourself to some time at a local spa. Or go to your hairdresser and indulge in a facial and a pedicure in addition to having your hair done.
- Find a massage therapist and get a nice, relaxing massage.
- Spend time with a friend—preferably one who doesn't have kids or has found someone to watch them for the afternoon! Go out for a nice long leisurely lunch in a restaurant that isn't family-style, someplace that serves interesting food that you enjoy, and have a nice long yakfest with your friend over a nice long leisurely lunch.
- If you're "playing hooky" from work while the kids are in school, tempt your husband to play hooky from his job simultaneously and

spend the day with you. Though you'll certainly want to spend some of that time making love when there are no kids in the house to over-hear you, get out of the house together, too. If the weather's nice, pack a picnic lunch and head for the beach or the park. Or go to a restaurant you've never tried before, or revisit an old favorite (possibly the place where you had your first date).

- Whether alone, with your husband, or with a friend, go to an art museum or some other place that pleases you but that you haven't been to in a long time (or ever) because it's not a place to take the kids.
- Turn up the stereo with *your* favorite music on—no rap, no *Barney* on the TV—curl up in your favorite chair, and reread your favorite book. Or, weather permitting, take the book out in the backyard with you. (Do your kids have a treehouse? Can you climb up into it your-self? Bring the book up there!)
- Go to a travel agency and grab an armful of brochures with which to plan your *next* R&R, which will be a weekend or a week out of town with your husband.
- Spend a weekend with your husband at a bed and breakfast that's nearby, so you won't have to spend much time travelling and can spend most of the weekend relaxing.
- Spend a long weekend on a Caribbean island, or at a ski resort, if that's more your speed.
- Take the whole family to a resort, one that offers child care for the kids, so you and your husband can go off and do your own thing together, whether that's swimming or golfing, tennis or sunbathing, snorkeling or boating, or walking around taking pictures, secure in the knowledge that the kids are being cared for—by someone else. Try to find a resort that also offers evening entertainment for the adults and evening coverage for the kids.
- Even if you take the kids away on vacation to someplace that doesn't offer child care, if it's a hotel or motel, you won't have to worry about doing dishes, making beds, emptying garbage, or reminding the kids to do chores or homework, so it's still going to be a vacation. Yes, there'll still be sibling squabbling, and yes, you'll have to remind the kids about everything from manners to bedtimes, but there's surely going to be a heck of a lot less friction than usual. And that's certainly a break from your usual routine—and a vacation!

13

THE BENEFITS
PACKAGE

Being a mom may be the most important job a woman will ever have (see chapter 1), but it's also likely to be the toughest—and the least remunerative. Just for the heck of it, figure out what it would cost you if you hired, at the going rate in your area, a nanny or other caregiver to take care of the kids. Now multiply that by the number of years you would need her services. See how much money you've saved? *And see how much money you would have earned if you'd been doing for someone else, for pay, what you do for your own family for free!* No, being a mom is definitely not remunerative, and it definitely should be.

Nevertheless, motherhood does have its rewards. There's no "golden parachute," but there *are* benefits and satisfactions.

Chief among them is the joy of watching your kids grow up into happy, productive individuals, and knowing *you* get most of the credit. Dad helped. The kids' teachers, Scout leaders, grandparents, even babysitters and others get some of the credit. Whoever else was instrumental in shaping them and helping them and being there for them also gets some credit. But *you*, Mom, get most of the credit, and rightfully.

Just as a CEO who has brought a company to success financially and in other terms (such as being a recognizable brand in the public eye) can properly take a large share of the credit for the company's accomplishments, you can take a large share of the credit if your kids turned out well.

I am not speaking of whether the kids turned out to be rocket scientists or musical geniuses or discoverers of the next lifesaving vaccine. I am talking about something much less earthshaking and yet much more profound: Did they turn out to have good personalities, good characters, good integrity and morals? Do they have satisfying careers, or are they on a career track as they go through school? Do they have friends they can count on? *Are you and your husband proud of them, and happy with the people they've turned into?*

Then you have a lot to be proud of and to be happy about. And to take credit for. Yes, they did it themselves, but with your help all the way. *This is your compensation, your "pay," your benefits package. This is what you've been working so hard to achieve.*

And of course, even before the kids grow up, there are many rewards along the way. When Jonathan graduated from being a tree in the annual class play to being a sheep—a speaking role!—who helped him rehearse all those evenings? You! Who sat there in the audience, missing work so she could watch her boy onstage? You! Who sat there mouthing every word as he spoke his lines? You! Who breathed a sigh of relief when he got through his part without a hitch? You! Who thought that the strong applause at the end of the show had to be mostly for Jonathan, the best sheep who ever trod a stage? You, of course.

And you applauded louder than anyone, just as you did at his violin recital, even though he squeaked quite a bit and missed a few notes altogether. Just as you did at his sixth-grade graduation, when that silly mortarboard kept slipping over his eyes, and he tripped on his gown on the way down the aisle as the pianist thumped out "Pomp and Circumstance" with as much dignity as she could muster. You applauded just as if this were a Harvard graduation and not a graduation from Eisenhower Elementary.

And Jonathan knew it. And he felt good inside, even if he was embarrassed. He said, "Awww, Maaaaaa!" And he complained that you were making a fool of yourself and embarrassing him. But you knew that he was secretly pleased.

And you did the same for your other two kids, because you were just as proud of them.

There's a part of your benefits package right there.

Now, what about all the times you stayed up all night with a child who'd spiked a fever of 103.9 degrees? What about all the nights you kept a humidifier running to clear the nostrils of an infant with a stuffy nose?

What about the three trips to the E.R.? What about finding out, the hard way, about Jimmy's peanut allergy?

Your job as a mom doesn't offer you medical benefits, only medical challenges. But you've risen to every one of those challenges, and your kids are still alive and well.

And if one of them does happen to have a medical condition that's a particular challenge for him and for you, you've handled it, dealt with it, and taught him how to cope too.

Pat yourself on the back, Mom. You've risen above and beyond, and your child is all the better for it. In time to come he'll thank you for it, and deservedly. Take the credit. It's your due.

Your "benefits package" includes all this, plus the handmade Mother's Day, birthday, and Christmas cards that left fingerpaint all over the kitchen table (but warmth in your heart when you opened the card), the presents bought with money that was cadged from you under thinly veiled pretense (and spectacularly wrong for your tastes, but the love involved shone through clearly), and the pride you felt when Chris asked you, "Can I take two cookies next door to Ms. Monroe? She lives alone and she doesn't bake. I bet she'd like them, and she's a nice lady."

Your "benefits package" also includes daughters-in-law, sons-in-law, and grandkids (whom you can spoil, and allow to stay up past their bedtime, and give all the other privileges you cringed at when your own kids' grandparents gave those privileges to them).

And your "benefits package" includes snuggling with your husband at night, in the darkness of your bedroom, and murmuring, "I think the kids grew up pretty well, overall. Don't you?" And hearing him murmur back, "Yes, largely thanks to you."

Your benefits also include having the kids move out on their own, to leave you back where you started, with the person you love at least as much as you love your kids—your husband. Just you and him. Starting over again, a twosome in tandem, facing the world together, proud of what you've accomplished together in raising kids you can be proud of.

But you know *you* get the lion's share of the credit.

You're the mom. The CEO of the family "corporation."

14

RELINQUISHING AUTHORITY

True, there are some CEOs who, because of their own personality quirks, have to micro-manage the company. These executives are loath to let others make decisions and need to manage, or at least approve, even the least significant of decisions and all but the most routine of actions.

With the exception of this particular type of executive, though, a typical and successful executive takes great delight in seeing those who work under her grow into their roles. She congratulates the middle manager who takes the initiative at making decisions, who manages his department well without constantly seeking guidance from her or from others in positions over him, and who grows in capability and assumes ever greater reliability and responsibility. People like these are the leaders of tomorrow. She also takes pride in seeing the worker lower down the totem pole who comes up with a good idea, finds an effective means to cut costs, displays leadership abilities, and otherwise demonstrates a readiness to be promoted to middle management.

Rather than fearing that such people, left to run things without strict supervision, will make ghastly (and costly) mistakes, she takes great pleasure in seeing them stretch their capabilities, prove their worth, and take on ever increasing responsibility. She is pleased for her company, which will benefit from their increased ability and initiative. She is pleased for herself, as their increased initiative makes her job easier. She is pleased for these people themselves, who are growing into their roles and readying themselves for their roles of tomorrow. And last, she can take pride in the role she herself played in these people's growth, whether she has mentored them directly or simply given them a good atmosphere in which their abilities could flourish and their sense of responsibility grow.

One of a parent's prime goals with each child is to raise him or her to be self-determining, self-sufficient, and able to make good choices. Like the CEO who watches her people's abilities flourish, Mom, too, can take pleasure on several levels as her kids grow older and more responsible. First of all, the family will be a smoother-running and more cohesive unit. Second, Mom's own job becomes easier when Courtney begins making good choices and decisions, or when Zac takes it upon himself to buy gas for the family car after borrowing it, to come home early because the weather is bad and the roads are getting slick, and to offer to give his sister a ride as long as he's got the car. Third, she is pleased to see her kids turning out well, taking more responsibility and making better choices, because she knows they are acquiring the skills they will need to survive and do well as adults out in the world. And last, she can take pride in the large role she herself played in fostering these traits in her children.

Yet it's not always easy to know when a child has reached the point that Mom can start giving him or her more freedom. Past a child's infancy, micro-managing isn't usually the best choice of leadership style for Mom, but when is a child ready for greater freedom?

Freedom, and the opportunity to make choices, should come in increments and start early. The mom who allows her child to select his own snack from the fridge is offering a degree of freedom and an opportunity to make a good choice (or a bad one). She may give some guidance: "Take something healthy" or "Don't eat too much. Dinner will be in less than an hour." Or she may trust the child enough to leave it up to him. The mom who lets her child cross the street alone for the first time, or walk to the corner store alone for the first time, is giving the child a certain amount of new freedom and trusting the child to make good choices: to cross only when it's safe, to go straight to the store and back without suddenly deciding to go over to Chris's house and without talking to strangers.

The mom who allows her child to decide that he wants to go out and throw a ball around with the guys and leave his homework for later, "because I don't have that much to do and I can still get it done by bedtime," is allowing her son a certain amount of freedom and allowing him to make his own choice.

An allowance, too, offers lessons in freedom and in choice-making: How will the child spend her money? Will she spend it all the day she gets it? If she does, getting a quantity of comic books and candy to enjoy but now having no money left till next weekend's allowance, will she live with the consequences of her actions? Or will she be bugging Mom by Tuesday for some more money because she just has to have the game her friend offered to sell her?

Inevitably, as they spread their wings and test the waters, kids will make some wrong choices. But only by being given the opportunity to make choices and to live with the consequences of their actions can they learn. If Mom keeps a tight leash on Conner and never lets him make his own choices, he'll never have the opportunity to exercise his decision-making process. And when, one day, life does hand him the opportunity to make a big decision, he's likely to make a spectacularly wrong one. Like getting hold of some beer by using a fake ID and then driving in an impaired condition. Drunk on freedom even before he opens the first beer, he'll celebrate his newfound freedom in all the worst ways.

Mom shouldn't bail her kids out every time they make a wrong choice, either. Only by living with the consequences of their actions can they truly learn the lesson that they need to think things through before making a decision. This is not to say that parents should *never* bail a child out of trouble. Clearly there are times when a child is in over his head and needs help, and the parents ought to provide it. Sometimes a child gets into trouble through no fault of his own, such as when he is unjustly blamed. And there are serious kinds of trouble that a child shouldn't have to face alone—such as if he gets in trouble with the law.

Suppose your daughter and her friend go to a store, and the friend says, "Let's take a couple of these sweaters home without paying. We can do it. I've done it before."

Emily, your daughter, says, "No. That's stealing."

Her friend says, "It doesn't count when you steal from a big company. It's not like stealing from a person. Besides, they expect a certain number of people to take stuff. It's fun. Here, see how easy it is? Now, are you chickenshit, or are you gonna take that pink sweater? It would look real nice on you!"

Swayed by her friend's arguments and not wanting to be seen as a coward, Emily takes the sweater—and gets caught. The store insists on pressing charges, and Emily is booked for theft.

What are you going to do? Leave her in jail so she learns a lesson? Get her out of trouble by paying the bail and other legal costs plus the price of the sweater? Leaving her in jail is certainly harsh, yet if you simply get her out of her jam and hope she learned a lesson, the scare she received may not be enough to impress on her that shoplifting *is* stealing and stealing is wrong. Better to get her out of jail, give her a long and serious talking-to, and tell her that you expect her to pay you back for all the costs you incurred from the incident, and you also expect her to write a letter of apology to the store manager or owner.

What do you do when Michael gets a ticket for speeding? First of all, you make him pay it out of his own money. (If he hasn't enough money saved up to cover it, you advance him the money and withhold part of his allowance every week till it's covered, or you let him work off part of the advance with extra chores, or you tell him to take an after-school job to earn the money with which to pay off the advance.)

What do you do when Keith, allowed to stay home alone one evening, invites four friends in despite your telling him he was not to have anyone over? Not only that, but they order a pizza, eat it in the living room (another no-no), and drop a piece on the sofa, staining it. After a serious talk on responsibility, obedience, and trust, you tell him it will be at least three months before you'll allow him to stay alone in the evening again. He may think he's too old to need a sitter, you tell him, but he's proven himself that he does need supervision, that he can't be trusted alone. "Maybe we'll try again in another three months or so, when you're three months older and wiser, but till then, you're still having a sitter when we go out in the evening." Hopefully Keith will learn from his own misdeeds and work harder to earn your trust next time.

How strong your response is should of course be commensurate with how serious your child's lapse in judgment was and how serious the consequences are or could have been. Generally, the best response is a talk and a revocation of the freedom that the child abused or misused. And when I say "talk" I mean "talk," not "lecture." Lectures are something kids—and most of us of any age—try to tune out. Better to have a talk in which you ask such questions as, "What do you think might have happened if ___?" and "What do you think would have been a better decision on your part?" and "Why do you think you made the wrong choice?"

Expect that your child will mess up from time to time. It's part of the learning process. But by your giving him freedom in increments, with little matters at an early age and more important matters as he grows older, hopefully he will make more of his errors in judgment in smaller and less important matters—like delaying his homework and then not getting it done in time for bed—and will have learned to exercise better judgment by the time he's faced with bigger decisions that bear more serious consequences for a wrong choice.

15

RETIREMENT—
OR YOUR NEXT CAREER?

There is a reason that some moms won't give their kids the freedom to make decisions and won't relinquish more and more authority to allow their kids a great amount of self-determination. It goes beyond the need to micro-manage. It goes beyond fear that the child will commit a serious error in judgment with serious consequences. It has to do with the mother herself, and her need to feel needed.

If you have invested most of your time, energy, and effort into the kids for the last sixteen or twenty-two years—and this is especially true of stay-at-home moms who don't have a career concurrent with motherhood—you are likely to feel lost when the kids no longer need you.

We're all familiar with the term "empty nest syndrome," but the reality is that many moms begin suffering from feelings of loss and depression before the kids even leave. The feelings start to set in as the kids begin to become more independent. The mother who has dedicated her life for the last two decades or thereabouts to taking care of her kids now finds she isn't needed as much. Though she may have complained about having no freedom, having no free time, being constantly on call and playing taxi driver, nurse, cook, and maid, suddenly the kids are solving their own problems, meeting their own needs, and Mom feels useless.

Now that she has all the free time she'd previously mourned the lack of, she doesn't know what to do with it. And it only gets worse when the last child has moved out or gone off to college and she's no longer heading up a family under her roof.

"Empty nest syndrome" isn't that different from the depression some corporate CEOs feel on stepping down from their leadership roles. What do CEOs do when they're no longer heading up companies? Some devote more time to their families; others devote more time to their hobbies, or develop new ones; still others seek new positions with other corporations, or a CEO may start a new business of her own, building it from the ground up.

What can a mother do when her kids have all grown up and she's no longer needed to be an active mom?

- Become a foster parent, or adopt, and start over again—not necessarily with an infant.
- Get involved in a program such as Big Sisters, in which she's involved in relating to and mentoring a child, but it isn't a full-time commitment, or in a Guardian ad Litem program or other volunteer program in which she works with children who need her.
- Become a Scout leader.
- Volunteer in her local school.
- Do volunteer work that doesn't necessarily involve children, such as tutoring adults who don't know how to read.
- Become a doting grandma when her kids present her with grandkids.
- Go back to work, if she's been a stay-at-home mom.
- Change careers or move up the ladder with her present employer, if she's working, now that she can devote more time and energy to her career.
- Start her own business, whether it's in a field she's worked in previously, or she's turning her hobby into a business, or she's striking out in a whole new direction.
- Get involved more deeply in her hobby or hobbies, or pursue a new one.
- Travel.
- Go back to school, whether to study courses that will help her advance in her present career, to learn things that will enable her to better change careers, or simply to expand her knowledge and make her a better-informed or more well-rounded person.
- Rededicate herself to her husband and rediscover the joy of "just us two" again.

You've raised your kids. Your job is slacking off. (It's never really completely over. They're still your kids, and even when they're in their forties and beyond, they're going to love you and occasionally need you.) But though the biggest part of your job as a mother is over, your *life* isn't over. So shake off those doldrums.

You've grown accustomed to heading up the family organization. You've run the family like a business and used your business skills, your organizational skills, for the good of your kids, your husband, and yourself. Now put those skills to good use in a different direction, if you want. Or go into "retirement" and pursue your hobbies, if you prefer. (You deserve it.)

But either way, don't forget to pat yourself on the back for a job well done.

You won't get a retirement package, a golden parachute, or a testimonial banquet. But you can look at your kids with pride, and you can see them look back at you with love.

And that's a pretty big reward.

RESOURCES
FOR MOMS

Websites

www.allaboutmoms.com/
www.organizetips.com/momandbaby.htm
http://aboverubies.org/articles/Others/TimeMgmtTipsForBusyMothers.html
www.mothersandmore.org/
www.spencerandwaters.com/resources.html
www.mothersoughttohaveequalrights.org/
www.athomemothers.com/
www.hbwm.com/
www.betweenfriends.org/
www.mommytips.com/
www.aimingatmoms.com/

Books

The Discipline Book: How to Have a Better-Behaved Child From Birth to Age Ten, by Martha and William Sears (Little, Brown, 1995).

What Every Mom Needs, by Elisa Morgan and Carol Kuykendall (Zondervan Publishing, 1998).

The Power of a Positive Mom, by Karol Ladd (Howard Publishing, 2001).

The Single Mother's Book: A Practical Guide to Managing Your Children, Career, Home, Finances, and Everything Else, by Joan Anderson (Peachtree Publications, 1990).

Mompreneurs: A Mother's Practical Step-by-Step Guide to Work-at-Home Success, by Patricia Cobe and Ellen H. Parlapiano (Perigee, 2002).

The Mother Trip: Hip Mama's Guide to Staying Sane in the Chaos of Motherhood, by Ariel Gore and Ellen Forney (Seal Press, 2000).

Organize Your Home!: Revised Simple Routines for Managing Your Household, by Ronnie Eisenberg (Hyperion, 1999).

Organize Your Family!: Simple Routines That Work for You and Your Kids, by Ronnie Eisenberg and Kate Kelly (Hyperion, 1993).